VARIOUS

CHRISTIAN

TOPICS

I0150011

VOLUME 1

9 Topics

HIS GRACE BISHOP MACARIOUS
OF EL MINYA, EGYPT

THE PARTHENOS PRESS

Various Christian Topics

Designed & Published by:
The Parthenos Press
101 S Vista Dr, Sandia, TX 78383
theparthenospress.com

CONTENTS

1

Sanctifying the Moment

An introduction about sanctifying the present moment

Thinking about the past troubles us. The bitterness and failure of our past makes us feel regret and we wallow in low self-esteem and lack of self-confidence.

Thinking about the future—the uncertainty of our success and contentment therein, our hopes, and the fulfillment of our goals and ambitions—worries us.

Meanwhile, **the *present* is lost.**

The present, which is more important, is lost. Yesterday has passed with all that happened in it and has become only a memory. Tomorrow, likewise, we do not own and we do not know, because it is in the hand of God. All we have is the present. We own the present.

May our past turn into a memory and an experience to aid us in the present. Also the future, may it become an enlightening hope, a beautiful encouragement, and a confidence in God that He will arrange what is best for us.

+ + +

Our dialogue here is about *the present,* which is certain—if it is even possible to be certain about anything other than God.

The past is gone, whether filled with good or evil, whether full of gain or loss, it becomes a mere memory.[1]

If we sinned in the past, God has forgiven us our past and consumed it, along with its evil, treachery, and weakness. He has covered this past with a veil and it has become as if it never was...Did we not repent of it?! Did we not confess it?! Therefore, the past has no remnant, no influence, and no authority. St. John Saba, known as "the spiritual elder" said, "Repentance transforms adulteresses into virgins" as if they had not sinned at all. "Come now, and let us reason together, says the LORD, 'Though your sins are like scarlet, they shall be as white as snow; though they are red like crimson, they shall be as wool" (Is 1:18).

We cannot recover the past; and thus we cannot mend or correct it. No longer is the past in our hands, it has become history. However, we can make *today* better.

When evaluating ourselves, we examine our past and extract experiences with regret for our wrongdoings; however, in order for self-evaluation to be constructive, we need to make the *present* better as a result of this regret. For this reason, we should not only have regret, but rather a mixture of self-reproach and hope. The self-reproach is for our

---

[1] There is a difference between remembering our past and allowing ourselves to relive it through our emotions. Our memories may stay active towards particular incidents, while our emotions concerning the same incident may gradually become weaker and cease overtime.

ignorance, weakness and lapses, while our hope is for improving the present.

What is important is that you are alive today; you awoke from sleep and a new day, full of hope, was granted to you. Imagine that you woke up in the morning to find that God, as a generous father, is handing you your daily allowance so you may commute. God does not give you a few dollars, but a whole unit of time—24 hours—for you to accomplish in it what you could not accomplish yesterday, because God's mercies are renewed every day. "This I recall to my mind; therefore, I have hope. Through the LORD's mercies we are not consumed, because His compassions fail not. They are new every morning; Great is Your faithfulness" (Lam 3:21-23).

It is as if God recreates time daily.

There is a Jewish saying that says, "three things cannot be retrieved: an arrow that was shot, a word spoken and a lost opportunity."

Though, it is wonderful to be satisfied with our past without regret. Whether we succeeded or failed, God will always make all things work for our best, regardless of cause or motive and regardless of outcome.

Yesterday we succeeded in doing good, ... today the good is twofold.

Having said this, it is necessary that we do not detach ourselves from our past, because we learn from the past. Therefore, it is essential to have a connection between the past, the present and the future, such connection as faith, ethics and moral principles.

Here, we will discuss purifying the present, being sincere in doing so, and taking pleasure in it.

Maybe we failed yesterday ... today we will acknowledge that failure.

What does the future mean for us?

Is the future a source of worrying that snatches us out of the joy of the present and causes us to be anxious?

Our lives need understanding, acceptance and adaptation, and since we cannot determine how the future will unfold, we must make every effort to purify the present moment and make it as constructive and joyfully beneficial as possible.

There is a Jewish saying that says, "Do not worry about tomorrow's troubles, because you do not know what will happen today. Perhaps you may not be alive tomorrow and thus you would have worried yourself about a world that never existed."[2]

Whenever you are troubled by thoughts of the future and assurance of success and comfort therein, cry out in your depths immediately, saying "GOD IS MY ASSURANCE," because the abundance of wealth and physical strength do not guarantee tomorrow's happiness. Likewise, neither promises of rulers nor pledges of the strong can guarantee the good we desire, nor the stability we seek. "Do not put your trust in princes, nor in a son of man, in whom there is no help. His spirit departs, he returns to his earth; In that very day his plans perish" (Ps 146:3-4).

If we wear ourselves out today in order to hoard money to enjoy tomorrow, then surely we will tire ourselves again tomorrow for the same reason. We will continuously exhaust ourselves as if running towards a tempting mirage.[3]

---

[2] Interpretation of Matthew 6:34 / William Barkley
[3] (ON TEMPTING MIRAGE): As if one repeatedly takes a spool of yarn and throws it with all his might, only to run to it, pick it up, and throw it again.

"Jesus Christ is the same yesterday, today, and forever" (Hebrews 13:8). God is unchangeable, and He Himself ensures to look after everyone who puts their hope and trust in Him, as when He declares with His pure mouth, "Because he has set his love upon Me, therefore I will deliver him; I will set him on high, because he has known My name" (Ps 91:14).

We believe that God is able to make the future a bright, joyful, and fruitful one, therefore we should live day by day, because many affairs belong to tomorrow and perhaps, if we know them today, we would lose our peace and bring upon ourselves grief. As Ezra the prophet says, "ordinance of each day" (Ezra 3:4).

It is not proper to waste our energy on regret over yesterday and anxiety over tomorrow. Yesterday should be let go of, as a dream and a memory, while we hope for an optimistic tomorrow, in order to invest our energy to excel in the present.

The wise said," Do not regret yesterday and do not worry over tomorrow so you do not miss out on the beauty of today." As Christians, we say, "Do not regret yesterday and do not worry over tomorrow, but be mindful in the present moment for your salvation."

Sanctifying the Moment

We own today. We have the ability to act today, and thus sanctify this very day. Today is our responsibility and we will give an account of it; if we live it as we should, then we can be assured that we can sanctify our entire life.

Life consists of units and each day represents one unit. Is it possible to separate today from yesterday and likewise from tomorrow, so that we can live each unit (day) independently in holiness and joy?

Can we separate today from our past and our future and turn into an effective unit?

Finding joy in every piece of bread we eat...

 .... Every cup of water we drink

 .... Every kind person we meet

 .... Every good deed we do

 .... Every useful piece of information we learn

 .... Every quiet night we sleep

In the book Way of the Pilgrim, the Russian Pilgrim says, "the trees, the plants, the birds, the earth, the air and the light all told me that they came into existence for the sake of the human and that they witness God's love to mankind. all of those things prayed and praised for God's glory."

As life itself has an ultimate goal, it also consists of intermediate goals for each stage of life. Keeping in mind this ultimate goal, we must live each of these intermediate stages to its fullness.

We may enjoy studying when our goal is to move up; because it is the means by which we reach that goal, and thus we may even study without feeling down or depressed since we have in front of us the hope of a relief that awaits us after graduation (when we begin our careers). The same joy, likewise, should be applied to our careers, church services, etc.

It is worth mentioning that enjoying what one does has an important role in their success. If one is convinced of the work he does, this will lead to many fruits and a guaranteed success. For example, the love of scientific material and general knowledge makes schoolwork an easy and very enjoyable task. The same applies to work, raising children and to other different aspects of life.

Sanctifying the moment is not Epicureanism

Epicurean philosophy denies the idea of immortality and rejects teachings about eternal life. Epicureans promote the idea of satisfying themselves with worldly pleasures as much as possible each day, as if there is no tomorrow. In contrast, in this discussion, we focus on sanctifying the present moment—sanctifying the day, every day, all day, day by day.

Epicureanism is cynical and expects evil, poverty, and war tomorrow. However, we sanctify tomorrow by sanctifying today, so that the days we have sanctified and consecrated—the days we have lived in holiness and righteousness—are transformed into a holy and fruitful life. Happiness lies in controlling our desires, not in indulging in our pleasures.[4]

We Desire to Taste Eternal Life

---

[4] The Epicurean philosophy belongs to Epicurus the philosopher, who was born in Samos in the year 340B.C. and died 270B.C. He first taught in Asia Minor and then Athens. His philosophy was developed during politically and socially unstable times which were the cause of anxiety and restlessness, thus he preached the idea to "enjoy the day." The pleasure which the Epicureans sought was a dangerous selfish pleasure that also denied eternal life and immortality, thus St. Paul the Apostle opposed this teaching.

The eternal life that we desire and we live preparing and longing for is not only expected in the future, but it is also a life that we live here on earth—at least this is what we are supposed to do. Eternal life is a tangible present and a guaranteed future.

We begin tasting eternal life here on earth because God is with us and as He said to us "indeed the kingdom of God is within you" (Luke 17:21). Having said this, our Lord also taught us to pray, saying "Your kingdom come" (Matthew 6:10), showing us that the fullness of His kingdom will be after this life on earth. Both here and in heaven, the common factor is that God is and will be the center of our life: "this is eternal life, that they may know You, the only true God, and Jesus Christ whom You have sent" (John 17:3). Therefore, we can say that if eternal life were a book, then our life here on earth is the book's introduction.

There is a thread that ties the creation of man and all the stages of salvation throughout the Old Testament, New Testament and forever. God Himself values and utilizes every moment for our salvation, and thus we should sanctify every moment for Him.

It is inappropriate to spend our time depressed, in anguish and worrying—should we despair today while waiting for tomorrow's good? No; today is beautiful, and whoever cannot enjoy today will not be able to enjoy tomorrow because life's beauty lies in the few hours we are living now; if wasted, then we have lost life entirely.

Read what was written by a virtuous man:

Look at this day

It is life... the essence of life

In its' few hours lie the reality of your existence.

The miracle of growth

The glory of work

The splendor of productivity

Yesterday is but a dream

Tomorrow is but an imagination

But if we live today as we should

Then it will make a joyful dream out of yesterday

And it will make a hopeful imagination out of tomorrow...

The Present's Salvation

Can we separate today from yesterday and from tomorrow as if life consists of today alone? As if you only get one *today* to live? Let it then be an ideal *today*! Do not let today be connected to yesterday nor an introduction for tomorrow, but seek with all your strength to gain salvation today...seek to gain salvation *now*...

You are responsible for today...you will be judged for it just as you will be judged for every day.

When our time of departure comes, we will be taken in whatever state we are in and will be judged accordingly. If your thoughts tell you to rest today and pray tomorrow, do not be deceived, but pray today because whoever does not pray today cannot guarantee that he will pray tomorrow.

"An elder's thoughts told him regarding fasting: 'eat today and fast tomorrow,' so he answered them, "No, that will not happen. I will fast today and let God's will be done tomorrow."[5] Mother Sarah also said, "Whoever does not give alms from one penny, will not be able to give from one hundred dollars."[6]

Therefore, whenever your thoughts begin to trick you suggesting that it is possible to be in better condition tomorrow than you are today, do not believe or listen to them because your thoughts tried to deceive you yesterday and they are using the same trap today.

Many times the difference between intense yearning for any spiritual deed and the loss of that same yearning is a thin thread of mere seconds. One may start to strongly long for a desire to do the good deed, be fruitful, and gain the expected comfort and joy from doing any spiritual deed, but due to the short delay, the desire has escaped one's grasp and is no longer there.

Work today, with all your strength, as long as you have the ability to work, because there will come a time when you will not be able to work. You have the ability today to give and to struggle although you may not have the desire to do so, however, tomorrow will come when you will have the desire, but no longer have the ability. Be watchful, "work the works...while it is day; the night is coming when no one can work" (John 9:4).

A wealthy man wanted to teach his children to be diligent, and so he told them, "Do you know how I've become rich? If you listen to my advice, you too will become like me." The children asked what the advice was and the father said, "Every year there is one particular day on which, if you work hard, you will become rich, however, because I am old I forgot which day it is. Therefore, do not be lazy in working hard

---

[5] Arabic Paradise of the Fathers p.339
[6] Arabic Paradise of the Fathers

every day because if you don't, you will miss out on the special day that makes you rich and you will lose the whole years' worth of hard work." Likewise, we also do not know the day of our departure, so if we become lazy we will lose all of our hard work and not reach our goal, but if we diligently struggle unto the end, we will find eternal life.[7]

From here also comes the precious advice of our teacher St. Paul of "redeeming the time," [Ephesians 5:16; 2 Corinthians 4:5]. By this, he means converting time: using it to pray, to serve, to do acts of love, to read spiritual books, therefore sanctifying the time and making it become of value. Those times are when we are truly living—the time we spend in fruitful, constructive, and effective deeds.

It is possible for a person to live fifty years but produce no fruits and therefore it is counted as nothing! There are people who lived and died without leaving behind any traces, but on the other hand, there are people such as St. John the Baptist who served for only six months but this short time was equal to years of service because of the fruits it bore.

It is the deception of the devil that forces you to think of and regret the past. He makes you waste time and effort in unwarranted self-blame and whenever you have finally stopped thinking of the past, the devil slowly lures you into worrying about the future.

There is much to know and enjoy today. Life is far too precious to waste in vain self-reproach or destructive anxiety. The lives of our fathers, the monastic elders and great ascetics, are an example of a deep self-awareness that did not allow their conscience to deceptively trouble them. In spite of spending long hours worshiping, doing hundreds of prostrations, praying and praising, fasting, in self-discipline and controlling their senses, they were full of joy and happiness. Abba

---

[7] Arabic Paradise of the Fathers, p. 209

Apollo says, "Why strive with sad faces? Are we not heirs of eternal life? Leave sadness and gloominess to idol worshippers, and wailing to the sinners, but the righteous and the saints should be joyful and delighted because they enjoy spirituality."

Look at how enlightened this father is. Abba Apollo's constant cheerful demeanor brought many to the ascetic life –a life of inner joy with Christ who Himself fills our hearts.

Conclusion:

Make today better than yesterday

And tomorrow better than today

We are in the hands of God and all we have to do is continue with Him without glancing at the past or looking at the future. We must be like children who are not easily preoccupied—neither bothered by the future nor dwelling on the past—but their only concern is to be beside their mother, enjoying her love while feeling safe in her protection.

Therefore, only the present moment deserves attention because it contains precious treasures. Imagination will only ruin your happiness and destroy your peace. It will make you relive the pain of the past and increase its bitterness. The future is in the hands of God and it is not good to pessimistically create a snowball effect of every bad possibility one may encounter therein. It will seem as if all the rocks on a path were gathered into a huge pile, blocking the road and obstructing one's vision, thus making you feel depressed and discouraged. A little effort every day prevents these rocks from piling up and thus enables us to continue on the path day after day.[8]

---

[8] In his book <u>The Gift of Oneself</u>, Joseph Shivers says, "The present is: A God-given opportunity that we may offer back to God, a duty to be fulfilled, an anguish to be endured, and sometimes a short respite under the eyes of God."

2

Life of Submission

At a time dominated by "practical atheism,"[9] it will be difficult to speak about a subject like submission, for some might look at it as being merely intellectual extravagance!

So, how do we submit to and trust a God we do not know?

Therefore, submission is a pleasant fruit of the fruits of faith. "Faith is confidence in what we hope for" (Hebrews 11:1), and not only what we perceive,[10] "and assurance about what we do not see" (Hebrews 11:1).

When the children of Israel complained against Moses in the wilderness,[11] because of the desire for food, God gave them manna and quails to satiety! "Now the Lord will give you meat, and you will eat it. You will not eat it for just one day, or two days, or five, ten or twenty days, but for a whole month—until it comes out of your nostrils and you loathe it" (Numbers 11:18-20). Then God returned to remind the

---

[9] This is besides the theoretical atheism wherein the atheist strives, through mind and reason, to prove that God does not exist.
[10] Sartre said: I believe in my body… in the Dollar… in the Bank… in what I perceive.
[11] Exodus 16:2

children of Israel that for the span of forty years in Sinai, He did not let their clothes wear out "your clothes did not wear out" (Deuteronomy 8:4). One of the theologians, in his meditation, states that God permitted their clothes to not wear out because they forgot to complain about clothes! This means that it would have been possible for them to not need food, if they had not complained about it. Consequently, had they complained about clothes and shoes, God would have given them with great abundance and generosity.[12]

Faith does not fulfill its work within the sphere of the possible; rather, at the point where a person's wisdom, cunningness and power ends, faith begins its work. That is, faith begins where the possible end, and sight and sense fail. Faith belittles difficulties!

The anxiety of young people is summed up in two points: *Lack of thanksgiving* and *lack of trust.*

The lack of thanksgiving for the current status with all aspects it might impose. It might be wealth status below what they desire, or a social status they are yearning to amend.

The lack of trust in God's ability to change the current status, or at least, change our attitude towards it; that is, He makes it suitable for us.

We ought to know that many of the wealthy are poor in thanksgiving. As well as many of the poor are loaded with grumbling!

We ought to compare ourselves with those who are below us in wealth and social status, and then thanksgiving will be stirred in us. And when we compare ourselves with those surpass us in spirituality, then humility will be stirred within us. Note that there must be two

---

[12] That is, the clothes of a child did not wear out but they were passed down to another child, and so on regarding the rest of clothes and rest of the people.

important reservations when comparing: in the first comparison, we need humility, and in the second, hope.

Our life, future and fate are in the hand of God alone.

We ought to trust that God will never let our life and our future be in someone else's hand or under another hidden power, no matter who or what. But He—glory be to Him—invests and moves all the human and material forces for the sake of accomplishing His good will for us. St. John Chrysostom[13] sees that even those, who want to cause us harm, will not succeed if we have trust in God that is equivalent to the faith of children. Moreover, there is a difference between someone trying to cause you harm, and you actually being harmed! Yes, there might be some who are striving to make you fall, but if you surrender to the harm, this is a different thing.

Was Abel harmed by Cain's hatred? No, but Abel was justified and Cain condemned. Was Joseph harmed by his brothers' envy? Of course not. For the harm of others does not harm us, but gives us redemption and makes us justified.

In the life of St. Macarius the Great, we find quite an amusing and amazing story. It was written that one time the devil attacked him, lunging at him with a great fearful force, intending on chopping his hand off with a knife he was holding. So the saint simply extended his hand before the devil calmly, firmly and humbly, and he said sweetly, "Go ahead, chop it off... for if God has given you permission to chop it off, will I be able to prevent you... but if the matter weren't so, then you

---

[13] In an articles titled "who can harm you?" [Arabic]

wouldn't be able to touch me..." And behold, the devil was transformed into smoke and disappeared.

This is the discernment of the saints.

This same affair happened with St. Anthony before,[14] when the devil tried more than once to hurt him, but could not, and this is because of his[15] trust in God and because he has submitted his life to Him.

God, in whom you have placed your trust, and to Whom, just as an innocent child, you have submitted the steering of your ship, will make your enemies "fight against you, but they shall not prevail against you. 'For I am with you,' says the Lord, 'to deliver you.'" (Jeremiah 1:19. Also Jeremiah 15:20)

Many of the presidents, governors, leaders, and custodians, in diverse fields, have found themselves driven by a hidden power to take some decisions, perhaps against their own wills, and found themselves willingly or unwillingly are pushed to take an action, because they are not the masters of themselves! But they are propelled to that for the sake of the good for God's children.

Perhaps this explains what we call: *grace in the eyes of others*.[16] That is, God gives you grace in the eyes of your superiors, moreover your enemies, and changes their hearts towards you without them having a clear reason! This is what David the Prophet expressed, when he said, "You prepare a table before me in the presence of my enemies." (Psalm 23:5)

---

[14] In time before St. Macarius
[15] That is, St. Anthony
[16] Also, "finding favor in the sight of others." See for example, Genesis 6:8; Exodus 33:12.

God has created in you a will, a desire, and a freedom, but when you submit to Him this will, He takes over the steering of your life, and leads it in the right path, even to the Kingdom.

Beware, however, that it is not appropriate to compare yourself with those who have succeeded after stumbling and those who have become rich after suffering, and those who have overcome hardships. God reproved, in the parable of the workers, the servant who envied his fellow servant who had worked for one hour and received the same wage. Though he worked for the whole day, the owner of the vineyard said to him, "Is your eye evil because I am good?" (Matthew 20:15)

God sometimes allows for a general decree to be issued to the benefit of *one* person who has submitted his life to Christ and trusted in Him. Was David's life in Saul's hand?! Never. The proof is that King Saul tried repeatedly to kill David but God saved him. Though David was steps away from Saul, yet Saul could not kill him. Saul was the king of Israel, while David was only a helpless young man, one of Saul's subjects, yet God preserved and saved him from a certain death, and made his life in the bundle of the living.[17]

The life of St. Athanasius the Apostolic was not in the hands of the Arians. He was in danger of death many times, but God preserved him and saved him from their schemes, and turned on them their evil. "But He has not given me over to death" (Psalm 118:18).

The martyrs as well, God preserved their souls and their spirits. For while the persecutors devised sophisticated methods to torture them, the martyrs mocked death in a way that amazed their persecutors exceedingly.

---

[17] 1 Samuel 25:29

The strugglers too, in deserts and mountains, in dens and caves of the earth,[18] God preserved them from becoming prey, and made the beasts be at peace with them, even serving them. He secured for them bread and clothing. The one whose leader is God, God becomes for him his bread, water, clothing, tranquility and safety.

In one of the porches of the Jewish Temple, herds of livestock, sparrows and other birds, used to be sold, along with whatever else the Jews needed to offer as a sacrifice. The sacrifice of purification for the poor was two sparrows.[19] Those who sold sparrows would sell two sparrows for a copper coin, and at times, to sway the buyers, they would sell five sparrows for two copper coins. Basically, a sparrow had no price! It's this same sparrow that the Master Christ spoke affirming that it is not forgotten before God, and that it will not fall without His permission, so of how much more value are we![20]

How many times have you desired your manager at work to be a just and compassionate person? And how often did students in university wish for a fair professor, or a dean who has a spirit of fatherhood? How many times did citizens wish that the officials in charge of their interests in governmental departments and agencies had mercy and forgiveness?

Now, rest assured, God is the One in charge of all these positions, for the reins of the matters are in His hand. Now you must root out of your heart all malice or hatred against anyone, for God is the Pantocrator.[21] "The king's heart is in the hand of the Lord" (Proverbs 21:1).

---

[18] Hebrews 11:38
[19] See Luke 2:24
[20] Luke 12:6, Matthew 10:29
[21] From Greek meaning Ruler of All

God, the Lover of mankind:

God loves His entire creation and the work of His hands, but no other creature is more pampered by Him as humans. He is a lover more than a master! He loved us and loves for us what is good, and loves that we live with Him in His Kingdom. He created us after creating for us everything, every good and all that is needed, that we may rejoice, and enjoy Him, and He with us.

Wickedness, however, which is in the world, is the product of man.[22] For who is setting ablaze wars and causing death and shedding the blood of thousands, and making others lose their homes and destroying their cities? Is it not man? He[23] abused freedom that he may destroy himself and make void his salvation.

Thanks be to the exceeding love of God for us, which compels Him to discipline us, prune us, and refine us, so that we may change to that image He desires us to become. So, do we submit to Him and trust Him when some discipline is laid upon us?

It is a strong test for submission ...

God is under no obligation to explain the reason every time He allows us to fall into trials or psychological stress. We are not able to question Him or condemn Him. "Would you indeed annul My judgment? Would you condemn Me that you may be justified?" (Job 40:8)

You ought to examine yourself and discover your weakness. As for God, He will explain at the right time. This is what the Lord said to our father Peter: "What I am doing you do not understand now, but you

---

[22] Genesis 6:5-8
[23] Man or the human being

will know after this." (John 13:7) So, will you be patient in silence, better yet, silent with thanksgiving?

We know only of the trials and the troubles from which God saved us, but we do not know about the many times God removed troubles from us before they came. Otherwise, who preserves you in your sleep, and on your way, and among the wicked?

But it seems that man's typical issue is forgetfulness.

God is the One who takes care of us.

Perhaps of the best metaphors, which the Divine Revelation used to describe the relationship between God and His people in the past, is the shepherd and the sheep. In the history of the early Church, the picture of Christ the Shepherd was found to be widespread on the walls of catacombs in Rome, and in early icons, in His beautiful simple form, carrying a sheep with gentleness and love, upon His shoulders.

One of the earliest symbols of God's shepherding care for His people is the sheep submitting[24] their life, in its entirety, to the shepherd. As for the sheep that relies on its intelligence and searches for other sources of food, then the wolf (devil) lies in wait for it among the forests.[25]

God does not care only for humans, but also for animals, plants and birds. He commanded for example to care for an ox, saying, "You shall not muzzle an ox while it treads out the grain." (Deuteronomy 25:4). Look at the splendid colors of plants and the sweet fruits: "And yet I say to you that even Solomon in all his glory was not arrayed like one of these." (Matthew 6:29. Also Luke 12:27)

---

[24] Also, surrendering.
[25] Literally, badlands. See Jeremiah 5:6.

Contemplate on the birds; see how God cares for them and gives them food, yet He declares with His pure mouth that we are better than the birds. "Do not worry about your life, what you will eat; nor about your body, what you will put on. Life is more than food, and the body is more than clothing." (Luke 12:22)

That is to say, if God has granted us the gift of life, will He be unable to give its sustenance? And if He has granted us the body, will He be unable to give it its clothing?! Yet, God is capable of preserving our bodies with no food, and He has granted many of the saints the ability to give up food for days and even many weeks.[26]

Abba Zosimas the Priest marveled at how St. Mary of Egypt could live in the desert without a garment! He even cast his cloak to her that she may cover herself with it. Fr. Paphnutius, the writer of the lives of the anchorites, marveled at how Abba Nopher's hair had grown so long that it eliminated the need of clothing.

Does clothing, therefore, and its abundance, profit anything? If they were put on a dead body, could they bring him back to life? The abundance of food and drink in the tombs of the Pharaohs, did they raise them up from the dead?!

The devil knows very well, more than anyone, that God takes care of His children and gives them sustenance and drives away all evil from them. But his war with them-that is the war of the devil-is nothing but to ridicule them, to make them doubt, and to weaken their trust in their Savior.

For the devil might incite a manager at work to mistreat one of his employees, and on the other hand he makes this employee have doubts

---

[26] Abba Pigimi the Anchorite fasted for eighty days; Abba Pishoy at one time also fasted for twenty-one days without interruption.

about God's love and care for him! But listen to what our teacher Paul the Apostle says, "For we are not ignorant of his devices." (2 Corinthians 2:11)

God deals with His children in two ways: either *fulfilling the need* or *dropping the need.*

With some people, God fulfills their needs of food, drink and clothing, patting them on their backs; while with others, He eliminates the need for them entirely. Consequently, the smaller amount of food is sufficient for them, and the simplest clothing covers. Said in another way, they are too occupied to sense the need of the body.

God's care, however, and His interest in His children, is not limited to food and clothing only, but it includes all life's aspects.

When you are in control:

The Jewish Talmud tells of a legend where Moses the Prophet asked God to let him undertake leading humanity, even for a single day! In the first hour of that day, Moses saw a man who had killed his friend, so he commanded that the guilty be executed immediately. At once God went to him, reminding him that he had killed a man once and He had forgiven him!

When you are the decision-maker in a whatever field, no matter how smart you may be, no matter how strong, and no matter how wealthy, you will not attain success as you would have attained when God is your leader and actual mover,[27] and when He participates with you in thinking, expressing, and deciding. The Bible says, "The horse is

---

[27] Acts 17:28

23

prepared for the day of battle, but deliverance is of the LORD."
(Proverbs 21:31)

You do not discern, in the same manner that God discerns, where
your benefit lies, and you will not love yourself as much God loves you.
There does not exist in the history of humanity someone who is more
intensely compassionate on human beings than God. David the
Prophet's heart was *after* God's heart, but he was never *like* God.[28]

It is said of Saint Macarius the Alexandrian that he went on a long
journey to visit some fathers. As he was walking, he feared losing the
path for his way back, so he began planting palm branches in the
ground, spacing them out, so that if he were to lose the way, he would
follow the branches to get back. On the first day of his journey, he got
tired at sunset, so he slept. To mock him, the devil gathered the palm-
tree sticks for him in a bundle, that he may put it under his head as a
pillow while he was sleeping. When he woke up from his sleep and saw
this bundle, he was troubled and distressed, and behold, a voice from
heaven said to him: If you have faith in the One who led the people in
the wilderness for forty years, then trust that He is able to guide you in
this short way. Truly, you must, as the Bible says, "lean not on your own
understanding." (Proverbs 3:5)

How many times did you lean on your own wisdom alone and the
results turned out disappointing? How many times did you take your
decisions, apart from God, and you returned from the spoil empty-
handed.[29]

Submission is to abide to the will of God and to trust in Him, like
an innocent child in his mother's arms, who does not care about

---

[28] See 1 Samuel 13:14 and Acts 13:22
[29] Lit. "in failure"

dangers, does not consider any emergency, and does not cower before any power. It is enough for him that he is with his mother. He has a deep feeling of peace, so that all danger and evil will not come close to him; confronting and overcoming danger is his mother's work alone.

Submission through the Cross:

Look at how the Son offered His will to the Father on the Cross, so that there may be for Them—or that He may declare that They have—a single will. "Not My will, but Yours, be done." (Luke 22:42)

Hide, therefore, in the Cross, and nail your will with Him, and endure affliction, sorrow,[30] reviling,[31] persecution,[32] and renouncement from your beloved[33]. Then you will arise with Him, in glory, joy and triumph, abolishing the enemy's accusation.

Submit your life to Him, and He will change your bitterness into sweetness and your weakness into hope and triumph. For He does above all that we ask or think.[34] He cures sicknesses,[35] repairs breaches,[36] and heals broken hearts.[37]

Think of how St Mary accepted the Annunciation, with Simon the Elder's prophecy that a sword will pierce through her own soul.[38] She said, "Behold the maidservant of the Lord! Let it be to me according to

---

[30] Matthew 26:38
[31] Matthew 27:44
[32] John 1:11
[33] See John 16:32
[34] See Ephesians 3:20
[35] See Matthew 4:23 and 9:35
[36] See Isaiah 58:12
[37] See Psalm 147:3 and Isaiah 61:1
[38] See Luke 2:35

your word." (Luke 1:38) The maidservant is a servant,[39] and the servant does not do his own will but does the will of his master. St Mary kept all these things and pondered them in her heart;[40] she accepted all that the Annunciation entailed, from leaving the Temple and being betrothed to Joseph, Joseph having doubts about her and his desire to put her away secretly, and more. As a result, with what honor was she covered and what blessedness did she receive—her praise on every mouth, and her glory, granted to her by her Son, received by no other.

Look at how our Father Abraham lived a life of submission. For when God called him to leave everything, even his kindred, he obeyed, without knowing the new place where God was moving him. Even when God asked him to offer his son as a sacrifice, he did not hold him back from Him! Moreover, Isaac himself did not complain nor object, but in a marvelous submission and innocence, he asked about the sacrifice. When his father placed him on the wood for sacrifice, he did not run away, though he was at that time twenty-five years old.[41]

So when Abraham submitted his life to God, God blessed him, and in him the nations were blessed[42]— He made him the root of the children of Israel. As for Isaac, who is a type of Christ, he lived a righteous life to a blessed old age, and in him a seed was called to Abraham: "For in Isaac your seed shall be called." (Genesis 21:12)

Between submission and dependence:

Submission, however, does not mean that we stand idly by, expecting God's work. There is a role we ought to do. In submission, the person performs his part completely, without any lacking nor negligence. He

[39] Lit. slave
[40] Luke 2:19
[41] See Genesis 22
[42] See Genesis 26:4

knows what it means to be faithful and earnest. Therefore, if he has fulfilled the role he is entrusted with completely, he will, without fail, accept afterwards the outcome which God will lay down for him, and he will rejoice over it without grumbling nor doubt.

As for dependence, it is when a person stands idly by, doing no work, without toil nor striving, without keeping watch, waiting on God to do everything. It is the dependent person also who often grumbles about what God has granted him!

But God has not taught us anything like that. He taught us, however, that we ought to invest our means and abilities, which He granted us, then He completes what is deficient. For in the miracle of feeding the multitudes, the Lord Christ asked His disciples to give food to the people, and only when they could bring a bit of bread and fish, as the utmost of their ability, He completed the work and fed five thousand men, besides women and children.[43]

Likewise, in the miracle of healing the man with the withered hand,[44] the Lord asked the sick to stretch out his hand. The man did not grumble though He had asked him to do the impossible—logic says he must be healed first and then he may move it. Nevertheless, he obeyed, and so was healed! When Christ raised Lazarus from the tomb, He asked the multitudes to take away the stone from the door of the tomb, though the One who is able to raise the dead, being God, is also able to take away the stone from where it was, by merely willing to do so.[45] The same teaching was repeated in the miracle of the healing of the blind. The Lord asked the sick to go wash in the pool of Siloam.[46] It is

---

[43] See Matthew 14
[44] See Matthew 12:13; Mark 3:5; Luke 6:10
[45] See John 11
[46] See John 9:7

participation in the work. For we do what can be done, and God does what cannot be done. St. John Chrysostom says, "God does not give the slothful, but He gives those who are unable to."

Moreover, in the Hebrew tradition, it is said that the water of the Jordan was not split so that the people may cross to the Promised Land, except after the bottom of the foot of the first priest touched the surface of the water!

Why anxiety?

Do not be anxious over school or work or shelter or marriage. For all who graduated were likewise anxious during school, and when others spoke to them about life of faith and submission, "their words seemed to them like idle tales." (Luke 24:11)

Moreover, all who attained eminent positions at work were anxious when they were diligently searching for work. All who got married and had children were anxious just like you, and see, they are dwelling safely with their established families. Nothing signifies more the necessity of trust and submission than the thousands of weddings that are celebrated every night in the churches!

For many have become wealthy, and thousands have excelled, of those who felt that they were a failure. Thousands of the weary have found rest. Napoleon Bonaparte ranked fortieth among his fellows at his graduation from military college. Albert Einstein, likewise, was weak in mathematics in his youth. Thomas Edison was an unknown child in early life, so that he had to move among several jobs to earn his living. And you may be one of these—and God comes at the right time and in the right way, and it is not right that we urge God to hasten in anything;

neither is it right that we dictate the way with which to solve our problems.

For in the parable of the virgins, [47] the virgins slept when the bridegroom was delayed in his coming. He actually was not delayed, as they had thought, but rather, they were wearied of waiting and wanted to hasten his arrival, so they slept! The bridegroom is coming at the appointed time, and no one can deter Him from coming; nothing will delay Him nor alter his plan.

Notice for example in the parable of the unjust judge, [48] how the judge was not willing to answer for a time despite the insistence of the widow, but at an appointed time he answered, not on the basis of the worthiness of the widow, but because of her perseverance. So God gives according to His compassion. Regarding this parable, Christ says, "Nevertheless, when the Son of Man comes (the time He answers), will He really find faith (trust and keeping watch) on the earth (in a man's heart)"?

Finally:

Even if you submitted your life and your affairs to God, you must submit them with no restriction or condition. For it is not becoming of you to specify to God the way with which He solves your problem. Instead, leave the whole matter to Him, submit your path to Him and leave Him to provide the solution He sees fit. For many pray "Thy will be done" with a reservation for a particular desire: they desire a specific manner to solve their problems. Even if you had your own desire or your

---

[47] See Matthew 25:1-13
[48] See Luke 18:1-8

own yearning, I wish you could place this yearning before God, without clinging to it.[49]

Pray to God, saying, "I see this matter, or I see this path suitable, but I care about learning Your opinion, Lord. If the matter were suitable for me, let me receive it from Your own hands so that I may rejoice in it as a blessed gift from You. If it is not suitable, I wish, Lord, that You remove from me the remembrance of it." Even the insistence itself-meaning the bold continuance-without feeling ashamed, is based on fulfilling God's will, not our own will. Supposing, for example, that you are thinking about monasticism, ask the Lord to split[50] a path for you to the monastery, to overcome the obstacles, to open the closed doors, and to give contentment to all parties; that is, when God sees that this path is suitable for you. Otherwise, let Him remove from you the thinking of it, and change your interest to another path. Again, the girl you see suitable for you to marry, pray about this fervently and with submission, that God may do what He sees suitable... and so on.

He who is living the life of submission has no desire but his eternal life, and before this desire, all other desires diminish, and even dissipate. He is a person whose eyes are open towards eternity and his mind unidirectional. Therefore, he disparages the present affairs, insults and loss, and even death.

Our teacher Peter the Apostle lay down sleeping in prison, while awaiting his beheading in the morning. He was neither afraid nor anxious, not even for his wife and children! He fell into such a deep sleep that the angel, when he came to save him, struck him to wake him

---

[49] The famous writer and literary figure Mikhail Naimy in one of his articles says, "We are sorry, God, that we give You many orders, of what we call prayer!"
[50] i.e. open up.

up![51] Peter's mind was not at rest, nor his heart calm, because God was going to solve his problem. No, not at all. Rather, he was joyful in the glory awaiting him in the morning, and because the whole matter was in God's hand.

God leads us Himself to Him for He is the Way, He is the How,[52] He is the Means, and He is the End.

He who has learned how to live the life of submission is a joyful person, for joy is the result of submission.

---

[51] See Acts 12:7
[52] Also, "manner" or "method."

3

Metanoia
(Prostrations)

Introduction

Metanoia is a Greek word which means repentance, transformation of intention, or revision of the conscience[53] towards God or towards others. The metanoia is made before God on an intimate level, and it is made before others as well, but on another different level.

Prostration is transformation in the mode of thought and feeling. Prostration is repentance, which is the transformation of mind and heart with regret.

In Greek, metanoia means:

- transformation of the mind and heart from earthly desires to Godly desire,

- transformation in the will to the direction of a new goal,

---

[53] In Coptic *ooshet* and in Greek *pro-ckun-hcic* and in English prostration

- transformation of the soul and the upper mind (which is of higher strength than the strength of the soul).

Moreover, metanoia in the Syrian and Hebrew languages means coming back and returning to the main position.[54]

Prostration in its form and prime meaning is an expression of repentance, admitting one's weakness and requesting forgiveness by dropping the body and letting the forehead touch the dust. It is also an expression of internal joy by the work of the Spirit, that is, the heart becomes fervent by the Spirit with overwhelming joy, which is followed by bowing down.

Perhaps, the word metanoia (prostration) comes from the Greek expression "*met-nos*," which means elevation above the mind [*meta* = above and *nos* = mind], which is what we cannot attain except by humility and submission with His grace.

"Therefore we praise Him and glorify Him with prayer and fasting and prostration before Him."

(Psali Watos / The Great Lent).

Prostrations and Spirituality

Prostration is an expression of groveling with contrite and utter submission and an expression of regret and desire of attaining blessing and forgiveness. When the forehead touches the ground, it remembers that it was created from the dust of the earth. This brings the mercies of

---

[54] Repentance in its patristic understanding in its hidden practice: Fr. Michail Negm, Alnoor Magazine, 2nd/3rd Edition p.80 / 1985.

God on the weakness of human nature. Prostration in its greatest portraits is being poured at the feet of Christ so that the worshiper submits all that he has of love, passion and gratitude. Prostration, then, becomes joyful and overwhelming with immense spiritual passion towards God. This is why the strugglers perform hundreds of prostrations at the feet of the crucified with overwhelming joy and great pleasure.

Metanoia is falling with Christ under the cross, then carrying it like Simon of Cyrene. It is also death followed by life (touching the ground then getting up), signifying everlasting life and resurrection with Christ, the resurrected from the dead. "For our citizenship is in heaven, from which we also eagerly wait for the Savior, the Lord Jesus Christ" (Philippians 3:20). In the liturgy of St. Serapion, there is a prayer of "bowing of the knees" prayed by the priest while the congregation is prostrating, which says, "we bow knees before you, conduct our thoughts, stretch forth your hand and get us up standing O Lord. Conduct us and help us to lift up our eyes and do not let us feel ashamed.[55]

When God eased the way of Eleazar of Damascus in choosing a wife for Isaac, he expressed his great joy by prostrating to God in thanksgiving and gratitude (Genesis 24:20). Here, we see how the work of repentance is delightful. A saint said, "As for me I shall pick myself up and go to where there is hardship."

St. Ephraim the Syrian said, "whenever a person is enlightened in prayer, they feel the necessity and the importance of prostration, and it pleases them to be steadfast in it. For whenever they raise their head in

---

[55] The Didache / The Liturgy of Serapion - The society of Theological Studies in the Middle East / p.87 1975.

fervency of heart, they are attracted to prostration for they feel strong aid with joy and bliss."

Prostrations in the inner chamber at the beginning of prayer enables the feeling of God's divine presence. The Levites prostrated with joy before God at the time of the sacrifice offering during the time of Hezekiah the king (2 Chronicles 29:30).

Prostration as a stand-alone spiritual practice

Prostration is a brief personal act of worship, and it is a practical recognition of the sovereignty of God and our submission to Him. Prostration, if accompanied by fear of God and humility, is a mere disciplined practice of worshiping God. Prostration is given as part of spiritual canons at times, especially for those who are not able to pray the Agpeya, accompanied with short prayers. St. Ephraim the Syrian said regarding this, "I love prostrations in prayer more than psalms; and when prayer gives you its hand, it rewards you for what you missed of your canon."[56]

If prayer is an offering to God as a sacrifice of mind and spirit, then fasting and prostration are an offering to God as sacrifice of the body, thus, the complete sanctification of the body, soul and mind.

Prostration is the means by which we express the shedding of our worries, troubles and burdens at the feet of Christ, who said, "Come to Me, all *you* who labor and are heavy laden, and I will give you rest" (Matthew 11:28).

---

[56] Saint Isaac means performing prostrations when bored with prayer - Saint Isaac's homilies / p. 133.

Who practice prostrations surrenders to Christ in a childlike innocence, and the worshiper says while prostrating, "Here I am, like a small child who cannot move, and is not able to get up, so take hold of my hand and raise me up and lead me, for my weakness has reached its depth, and I have no strength to stand up."

At other times, prostration is accompanied by feelings similar to the feelings of St Bishoy, the beloved of our good Savior, who desired so much to bow to wash Christ's feet again, and to kiss them with joy and reverence, so that he would find comfort and consolation.

Therefore, it is good for us to prostrate in front of the icon of the cross, to draw from it strength and hope that the One, who bore our sins and lifted our pains, is also able to save us from what weighs us down. "Surely He has borne our griefs and carried our sorrows" (Isaiah 53:4). Simon, the New Theologian, says about weakness and negligence, "Hasten to your usual place of worship and prostrate before God who is perfectly merciful and tender. Pray with a groaning, contrite heart, and with abundant tears, beseeching God to lift the burdens of weakness, despair, and evil thoughts. For if you keep knocking with contriteness without ceasing at the doors of God's mercy, He will open for you at once, and you will become like a righteous person.[57]

Saint Isaac adds that prostrations are suitable as a treatment as they are effective at fighting the forces of darkness, saying, "if it is a time of combat and gloom, and if we are bewildered, we will stand firm in prayer and in prostrations to the ground."

Moreover, prostration is a desire to know and submit to God's will so that we can humbly understand it and receive the heavenly gifts and blessings. St. Ambrose says, "We bend our knees, because bent knees,

---

[57] The Philokalia translation of Mr. Mikhail Tawfik 1973 / p.1123

more than anything else, entreats forgiveness from God, the removal of his wrath, and the acceptance of his blessing."[58]

St. Isaac says, "The continuous watch, with reading and continuous prostrations, incites granting of good things to the saints, and the one who finds talents only finds them through these things, and those who desire good things should be at peace working towards this."[59]

This is why prostrations have assumed a place and importance in the life of discipleship among the ascetic fathers. New monks practice prostrations as a sign of submission to the elder father and a desire to become his disciple. St. Paul (Boules) the Simple made a prostration before St. Anthony the Great, begging him to accept him as his disciple seeking his guidance and prayers. [60] Likewise, St. Maximus and Domadius prostrated when they met St. Macarius the Great, and again when he departed from their cave.[61] Also, in the life of St. Macarius of Alexandria, we read that a brother came and prostrated before him, saying: "Father, I ask you to accept me under your shadow." [62] Furthermore, the great elderly fathers also prostrated before those younger than them and with lesser ascetic experience, when they found something that would benefit them and help them in the salvation of their souls.[63]

Prostration is an invocation to God, when accompanied by the raising of hands and gazing towards heaven. When King Solomon inaugurated the temple of God, he kneeled and spread his hands

---

[58] The Life of Prayer, Fr. Matta Elmeskin (Matthew the Poor)
[59] The Ascetism of St. Isaac (Mar Ishaq) p. 48
[60] The Paradise of the Desert Fathers p. 22
[61] Paradise of the Desert Fathers p. 41 & 43
[62] Paradise of the Desert Fathers p. 347
[63] Revise the story of the elder who was rescued by his disciple, with his wisdom, from grudge and hatred; Paradise of the Desert Fathers p. 411.

towards heaven (2 Chronicles 6:13). Our teacher, Paul the Apostle, refers to supplication to God in prayer in (Ephesians 3:14, 16) and he himself kneeled while praying (Acts 20:36). St. Isaac says, "...and there are those who stay up all night supplicating with psalms, and those who work prostrations and prayers of reverence with bows to the earth."[64]

Worshipping in Spirit and Truth

St. Isaac says, "Do not think that prostrating before God is an easy matter, for none of the righteous deeds equal the perseverance in completing the service of prayer by striking prostrations." He then goes on to say, "Force yourself to prostrate before God because prostration stimulates the spirit of prayer."

When the Samaritan woman asked Jesus about true worship, the Lord draws her attention to a new type of prostration, which is in spirit and truth. He encouraged her to move from formal worship to a deep belief of the Divine Presence (John 4:23).

St. Isaac says, "when God moves your heart and makes it humble, keep doing continuous prostrations and worship, and do not let the heart care about any of the things that the demons command you to do. Nothing in the ascetic struggle is greater and more tiring than for a person to throw himself before the cross of Christ, which is something that the devils envy him for, and to devote himself night and day like a person handcuffed backwards. Then the light will shine in you from within, and your righteousness will shine quickly, and you will become like a flowering paradise and an inexhaustible spring of water."

---

[64] Asceticism of St. Ephraim the Syrian

Prostrations and Manners

Prostration is also practiced for sympathy, extinguishing the flame of anger, absorbing the charge of pride, and calming troubled feelings, provided that it is presented honestly and from a contrite heart. Abigail was able to calm David's wrath by prostrating before him, thus calming him and avoiding bloodshed and revenge (1 Samuel 25). David admired her wisdom. He did not consider her humility as weakness, and did not despise the sacrifice of her apology. Jacob also did the same when he prostrated to the ground seven times in front of his brother and dissipated the enmity that had been so strong between them (Genesis 33).

St. Isaac says, "There is none among the virtues loved by God, honored in the eyes of angels, which conquer demons, terrify the forces of darkness, grant knowledge, bring mercy, give humility and joy to the mind, more than prostrations before God."

When we prostrate before a person, our thoughts towards him change, and we change his thoughts towards us, and we drive out illusions and expel disturbing thoughts from him. St. Peter the Damascene says, "Quarrel is alien to the path of Christian life, as St. Paul the Apostle said, "But if anyone seems to be contentious, we have no such custom, nor *do* the churches of God" (1 Corinthians 11:16). In this way each of us knows that when we quarrel, we are outside the church and are strangers to God, and thus we need this wondrous work of repentance. But if repentance is not complete, not even a thousand prostration can help."[65]

In the writings of the fathers, we read about that good and wise brother who defeated the demon of anger by prostrating to his brother

---

[65] Paradise of the Fathers

who was fed up with him because of a simple mistake and begged him not to be upset. Palladius says, "God tormented that devil—who caused the crisis—until morning."

However, if you do a prostration routinely and not from the heart, the other will not accept it. St. Macarius the Great says, "Each of us has a way to know whether or not the other is truthful in what he says and in what he behaves!" The Roman soldiers prostrated before Jesus in the Praetorium, but for ridicule and disdain (Matthew 27:29).

Thus, a prostration is not sufficient as a way to resolve a situation, if it lacks sincere feelings of love and meekness. Actually, it may be an attempt to draw attention or to attract praise. The inner thought is more important than external appearance.

Saint Peter of Damascene says, from St Basil the Great, that with regard to expressing repentance to God or apologizing to others, the quantity of apologies will not help as much as the sincerity of the apology, because a thousand prostration made by a person in front of the other or before God, without a contrite repentant heart will not help as much as a one prostration with a repentant heart, saying: "Forgive me, my father (or my brother), for it is this." Thus, he will forgive, and that one prostration will eradicate strife.[66] In this manner, the prostration will be fruitful inasmuch as it contains love for God and for others.

A symbol of welcome, submission and sympathy

In the monastic rule, prostration is used (in addition to the above) to express sound monastic life. On one occasion, some of the clergy came

---

[66] Homilies of St. Isaac, p. 38

to St. Tadros of Scetis to accept the blessing of the priesthood. When he rejected because of his feeling of unworthiness, they made a prostration for him begging him to accept only to hold the chalice in the church (it is the right of the Deacon to hold the chalice and give of the blood of Christ to those who partake of it in the absence of another priest), but he apologized with the same kindness that they asked him.[67]

Likewise, the fathers when meeting each other, prostrate in reverence, where each one is humbled before the other, expressing his submission and his love. Saint Isaac says, "Be humble before all people, and you shall be raised above the rulers of this age. Initiate with salutation and prostration and you will be honored more than those who carry gifts of pure gold."[68]

When visiting each other, it was the custom of the fathers to greet each other with prostrations, followed by a period of silence of up to an hour! This tradition has biblical roots; Lot prostrated before the two angels when receiving them (Genesis 19:1). Likewise, at the meeting of David and Jonathan, they emotionally prostrated before one another with tears (Samuel 20:41).

In monastic tradition, it was customary when a disciple meets with his elder or when the monk meets with the abbot of the monastery, that he prostrates before him and not rise until the father raises him by bending down and raising him gently. We read in the Ladder of Divine Ascent [by John Climacus] that Saint Minas (Mena), when he prostrated before the head of the monastery, the father left him for a long time before setting him up reproaching him for his love of vainglory! When the fathers later asked him what he thought, he said

---

[67] Paradise of the Desert Fathers, p. 104
[68] Homilies of St. Isaac, p. 38

that he recited the entire book of Psalms while he was prostrating on the ground.

Thus, prostration is not only a bodily movement, but it is a movement of a contrite heart and a repentant conscience that presents itself as a living sacrifice to God, either in His holy temple or to His image in others. It starts internally saying "Why are you cast down, o my soul?" (Psalm 42:5).

Prostrations and Physical Health

Moreover, prostrations are beneficial to the body, though we do not treat them as a physical exercise. They are useful, especially in the morning, to promote blood circulation, and prepare the body to perform its daily activities. Today, physical therapists agree that prostrations benefit the body, making the body fit and ridding it from various diseases of the spine.

Anatomical view of the back:

The human back consists of the backbone and the spinal cord. The spine consists of 33 vertebrae, which serve as support for the body, for weight distribution and for shock absorbance. The vertebra consists of a main body and three spinal protuberances. The bodies of the vertebrae are stacked on top of each other, separated by a septum that is a cartilaginous disk, in what is known as the cartilage. This structure is supported from the outside by ligaments and muscles. All these parts are nourished by blood, except for the cartilaginous disc, which gets reduced blood flow after the age of ten. This disc may be exposed to premature wear, especially for those who live a sedentary life, in which no exercise or sport is practiced, as well as those who incurred injuries from incorrect movements and posture.

There are two mechanisms that occur when bending:

The first is called *rhythm lumber pelvic*. It occurs when the torso is bent forward in an attempt to touch the ground, so the lumbar vertebrae—at the bottom of the spine—bend forward about 45 degrees, and are followed by an automatic rotation of the pelvic bones.

The second is called *rhythm lumber Pelvic Reverse*; it is the opposite of the first mechanism, and it occurs when a person tries to return to his natural erect position, where the lumbar vertebrae return to isolation accompanied by reverse rotation of the pelvic bones. In both mechanisms, there is a continuous work of the muscles of the back and the upper back leg.

Thus, we notice the existence of a natural mechanical process of bending, and if any defect or disturbance occurs in one of these two mechanisms, then back problems will begin to appear.

These two mechanisms are achieved through two ways:

1) The knee is completely straight: when the person bends forward, the weight of the upper part leads to a curvilinear movement on the cartilage discs, resulting in an increase in the load on the spinal spurs of the lumbar vertebrae, which leads to pain in the lower back.

2) The knee is completely bent: it is noticed that when the worshiper begins the prayer by doing a prostration, he first bends his feet in the direction of his feet, as a result of the weight of the body. At the same time, he bends his knees completely, as he accompanies the "lumbar pelvic

reflexology" as mentioned above, so that his forehead touches the ground, and the prostrator uses his hands to reach the ground, which acts as a lever to get down and get up off the ground.

Flexed knee Mechanism:

When the worshiper bends his knees, he tightens all the muscles of the leg and back, in addition to moving his back vertebrae and joints between the vertebrae. This helps in avoiding early complications in the knee, such as (arthritis) and back pain, and therefore it protects from such troubles. Hence, the belief among some that prostration causes back and knee pain is incorrect when the prostration is performed in a correct manner, as indicated.

In addition to this, prostration works to strengthen the back muscles in two ways:

1) *Contraction Eccentric*: while descending to prostrate slowly (in the direction of gravity), the muscles contract - controlling the movement - away from its center.

2) *Contraction Concentric*: it is the normal contraction while ascending from a sitting position to a normal position. The muscles play a limited role in prostration, aided by gravity while descending. Prostration also plays an important role in the flexibility of the joints as it maintains the range of motion and even increases it in some cases, and also helps to strengthen and stretch some muscles - if they are pulled - especially the back muscles and the calf muscles.

This is in addition to what it plays in improving blood circulation to various parts of the body; improving breathing and increasing Vital Capacity.

During prostration, the intra-abdominal pressure increases, which increases the intrathoracic pressure, which helps with exhalation. On the other side, prostration helps with inhalation during the ascent.

Types of Prostration and its Practice

Prostration is a process of kneeling down and getting up. When the prostrator bends his knee, he feels within himself that he is humiliated by sin and raised from above. He repeats this according to the number that his spiritual father advises him. Here, the prostration represents the movement of life: the continuous struggle; with negligence we fall and by Christ we rise again.

St. Theoleptos, Metropolitan of Philadelphia says, "Do not neglect worship, for prostration expresses the soul that has fallen into sin, and confesses its sin. As for rising from prostration, it expresses repentance and a promise to follow the path of virtue. Make every prostration accompanied by a mental supplication to Christ." By falling before the Lord in spirit and body, we obtain the grace of the Lord in spirit and body."[69] During the prostration, it may be sufficient to pray the arrow prayer, such as the Jesus prayer (Oh my Lord Jesus Christ, have mercy on me, the sinner).

---

[69] Philokalia, V.4, p.185

Prostration has three forms:

1) <u>Bowing the head</u>: Simply bending the head while the person is standing, with two hands joined at the chest.

   This is what happens in the Divine Liturgy several times when the deacon calls to the people, "bow your heads to the Lord", whether when reading the absolution at the end of raising of incense, or when the people bow their heads at the time of the absolution the servants. Here, the church takes the position of the publican, who bowed his head out of shame for his sins, to cry afterwards, "One is the Holy Father..."

   We also bow our heads during our prayers in the inner chamber. Moreover, it is preferred that we bow the head in the presence of our elders out of respect, especially for spiritual fathers and guides.

2) <u>Kneeling</u>:

   This method is more widespread among the monks of the West, where it is called semi-prostration, i.e. half a prostration or partial prostration, in which the worshiper kneels on his knees, while his hands are raised up in the form of supplication, as the Lord Christ kneeled and prayed to the Father (Luke 22: 41), and as the young man kneeled to him, asking to know the way of the kingdom (Mark 10:17). The apostles began to practice this kind of prostration as well. St. Stephen knelt on his knees, praying to God not to hold the sin of his prosecutors (Acts 7:60). In the Old Testament, Daniel the Prophet knelt down in his cell, looking towards Jerusalem through the window, as was his habit every day (Daniel 6:10). After that, the worshiper begins to bend until his forehead touches the ground and then returns to the kneeling position, in repetition. He may continue to kneel in prayer like Solomon the Wise in the ritual of the consecration of the temple (1 Kings 8:54).

3) <u>Bowing Down (Full Prostration)</u>:

In Greek (Προc), which is full prostration, where the forehead touches the ground. The church practices this type of full prostration several times in the Divine Liturgy. For example, when the priest prays saying, "May your Holy Spirit rest upon us and on these offerings," the people do a full prostration. Also, when the priest raises the holy Body and says, "Holy body and blood," the people answer while prostrating, saying: "We worship your holy body and your precious blood... O Lord, have mercy." Also, the congregation prostrates once again at the end of the liturgy, at the last confession, which summarizes the faith of the Church in her incarnate Savior.

It is preferable for the worshiper to kneel down first and then bend forward, then get up in the same way, so that the large number of prostrations do not affect the health of the prostrator, especially his spine. There should be a short pause between a prostration and another, so that the worshiper does not run out of breath and his body is not quickly exhausted. Rather, prostrations should be made with grace, harmony and balance, with the worshiper's body completely straight when standing up.

It should be noticed when prostrating that the fist is joined so that the thumb and the lower third of the index finger are combined: the shape of the cross. This signifies readiness, will, strength, and worship.

Also, the hand bones would not be fatigued in this way. This is in comparison to the wrong way of prostrating by spreading the fingers.[70]

If the worshiper notices that the fingers have begun to stiffen at the end of the hindquarters on the back of the hand, he can then prostrate on the palm of the hand while maintaining the position of the hand as mentioned.

There is a new form of prostration, which has spread recently, and it is unfortunate and has no reference, neither in the Bible, nor in the tradition of the fathers. It is just bending over for the tips of the right fingers to touch the ground, in front of the temple or the relics of saints or bishops. Some justify this by the lack of time and the increase in numbers wishing to receive the blessing of the bishops

Hence, it is possible for the bishops to have a full ritual prostration inside the church, while outside the church it is sufficient to bow properly, but this should not be - that is, merely bending - the form of the prostration in the inner chamber.

And another form of prostration is practiced by a person when his soul is very bitter, as if he no longer has the strength to stand, request or invoke.

This is an expression of the greatness of his longing or the breaking of his heart. Behold, the Lord Christ, in his psychological suffering before the crucifixion, "my soul is very grieved to death" falls on his face

---

[70] There is an interesting tradition indicating that when the devil fell, he fell with his hands open! Perhaps there is a relationship between this idea and the icon of Archangel Michael trodding the devil with his feet, while the devil is fallen with hands open.

to the ground (Mark 14:35). Elijah the prophet expresses the utmost forms of psychological bitterness by falling down on the ground with his face between his knees (1 Kings 18:42). The leper, who was having a grim life and rejected by everyone, as soon as he saw Jesus, he fell on his face to the ground in front of Him (Luke 5:12). It is an attempt to seek God's mercies and forgiveness, and it always succeeds and bears fruit because God is overcome by our tears and our humility; "Turn your eyes away from me, for they have overcome me" (Song of Solomon 6:5).

St. Augustine says, "The one who prays should offer whatever parts of his body that can befit with the supplication, so he should kneel down and then...either spread his hands upwards or fall down on the ground."[71]

Other types of prostrations:

Prostrations are also made to the relics of the saints at any time of the day, in which honor is offered to the pure ones of God. Prostration of respect is seen in the Holy Bible, like the prostration of people before kings (the anointed of God). When Jacob met Esau after prostrating to him seven times, he said: "inasmuch as I have seen your face as though I had seen the face of God" (Genesis 33:10). David also prostrated before Saul ... etc.

And when we prostrate, for instance, before the relics of St. Moses the Strong, we say hail to St Moses the chosen of God and likewise

---

[71] Life of Prayer p. 207 from Decrum Pre-Martius

49

before the body of Saint John Kama, etc.[72] We see also, in the divine liturgy, that the priest comes out of the altar with incense. He stands in front of the sanctuary facing east, then says: we worship you, O Christ, with your good Father and the Holy Spirit, for You came and saved us. Then he bows and says, "But as for me, I will come into your house in the multitude of your mercy; In fear of You I will worship toward your holy temple." Then he bows and says: I will praise you before the angels, and bow down in worship toward your holy temple. Then he bends and turns towards the north and says hail to you, O full of grace, the Lord is with you....Hail to my lords and fathers the apostles. Hail to St John, while he also bows every time.

We also prostrate before the patriarchs and the bishops for veneration and respect as mentioned before; given that the bishop is a representative of the Lord Christ. Therefore, we celebrate (venerate) the bodies of the saints and receive them, as well as the bishops, with hymns that are originally directed to the Lord Christ Himself. Hymns such as the hymn of *Epooro* (O King of Peace), the hymn of *Ekezmaroot* (Blessed are You) and the hymn of *Eflogimenos* (Blessed is He); which are all hymns pertaining to God alone.

It is possible to prostrate before others whom we feel we have offended, which is often mentioned in the stories of the fathers. In it we are broken before the other and ask for forgiveness. Just like when we prostrate before God asking for forgiveness. We read a lot in the lives of the saints, the advice of the fathers for their disciples, "make a prostration for the brother... ask forgiveness...." This expression still continues today, where the sinner is asked to present a (repentance)

---

[72] God attributes himself to Abraham, and he says in the bush (I am the god of Abraham, Isaac and Jacob), and accordingly, even if we consider this prostration as worship, then we prostrate to the God of Abba Moses...etc.

prostration before the one who he sinned against. But if the offense was against the group of brothers, it was - and still is – asked of the sinner to stand at the door of the church to make a prostration before the others who enter or leave asking for forgiveness and prayer for him, with tears and humility. The purpose of this is to help him feel how shameful what was caused by him, and if it is painful here before people, then how shameful would it be there? The Fathers used to use such a "healing economy" especially in connection with the sins of pride. Also many of the fathers use this economy in case of falling into grim sins, as they link unclean thoughts and actions with pride, so they advise the sinner to perform a number of prostrations for several days accompanied by fasting and prayers. So with the humbleness of the body, the spirit would rise and the war would calm down. When St. Daniel of Shiheet (Scetis) sent one of the brothers, who was attacked by fornication, to a place where he could seclude himself and pray. The brother said, "I was constantly contrite and praying to God and prostrating" and he recovered from this war.[73]

But we should pay attention to the fact that the economy of prostration may turn into a punishment for some. Which leads to dire consequences, and its sweetness is lost and becomes a burden that one seeks to get rid of it.

Prostration number and timing

The way we explained (in full prostration) explains to us how the fathers used to make hundreds of prostrations, or sometimes thousands,

---

[73] Paradise of the Desert Fathers, p. 106.

in one day, without severe fatigue or abuse of the body, as the body is a talent that we must preserve.

Frequent prostration compliments prayer and vigil and it is bound to them in the spiritual life. For this we note that the midnight prayer is divided into three watches. St Isaac says, "We must fast, read, and stay awake in quietness all night long; and that is according to the ability of each one. The number of prostrations that are supposed to be done during the hours of the day as well as at night; we should do thirty prostrations at least each time, then we prostrate to the Holy Cross and rest. Whoever wants to add to this canon, should do as much as he can and according to the economy of his spiritual father. There are those who spend three hours reciting one prayer while their faces on the ground, in order to keep their mind calm without pressure or distraction. For prayer and prostration show the abundance of riches of the goodness and riches of grace granted to each person according to the degree of his worthiness."[74]

St. Isaac says about those who are advanced in the spirit, "It is recommended to prostrate always, and to be steadfast in it, even if one continues for three days, kneeling on the ground in prayer, the prostrator does not feel tired because of the sweetness and pleasure that he feels" *(An article in silence).*

We read about St. Christophorus that a monk prostrated before him begging him to tell him some of his experience. The saint told him how he used to visit the cave of St. Theodosius, and it had eighteen steps, and he used to prostrate one hundred times on each step, and when he reached the bottom of the cave he made many prostrations (of course

---

[74] The Homilies of St. Isaac, p. 50

several hundreds), and this continued for twenty years with intense spiritual struggle and asceticism.[75]

We read about the nun of the monastery of *Armeius* (St. Anna-Simon) how, after the other nuns slept, she rose to make many prostrations with tears and contrition. (...one watch of the night would not have passed until she would have gotten up and raised her hands towards heaven and opened her mouth and blessed God. She made many prostrations and her tears ran like a fountain.)

St. John Saba, known as the spiritual elder, says, "Loving continual prostration before God in prayer is a sign of the soul's death from the world and its awareness of the secret of the new life."

And in the abbeys and convents of Egypt today, there are monks and nuns who preform hundreds of prostrations per day; And some of them are over sixty years old, and some of them suffer from health issues (such as heart problems and diabetes) that can excuse them from performing prostrations. One of those used to do more than a hundred in the morning, and we used to hear him. If someone knocked on his door during that, he would go out cheerfully, not gloomy or exhausted. Another, who passed away a few years ago, used to prostrate three to five hundred times every morning, at sunrise. One morning, I knocked on the door of one of the elder monks, and he came out smiling at me. I was hurrying him to leave for an important matter; but because there was good friendship between us, he said to me with gentleness and meekness; leave me a little, I only have a few prostrations left! And when I asked after that about the number of prostrations which this father

---

[75] The Paradise of the Desert Fathers, p.234; some fathers believe that the number of prostrations mentioned is exaggerated.

made, I was told that it is three hundred prostrations. I was amazed at that because he was over sixty years old.

St. Isaac advises to stay awake until midnight with uninterrupted prayers, with the service of the psalms, performing of prostrations, bowing down, with elated prayer, the supplication of the heart, and the stretching of the hands towards heaven.[76]

But the matter needs to be gradual. Let the beginner start with twelve prostrations, arranging this with the spiritual father. If the father of confession is one of those who pity their children from fatigue, then it is up to the worshiper himself to reveal his desire to his father of confession in longing to taste the sweetness of prostration; provided that the number does not exceed the number agreed upon without referring to his father of confession, and after a period of no less than a year from the beginning of practicing the original number.

One of the blessed fathers, when asked about the number of prostrations that a person can begin with in his spiritual struggle, says that it is possible for a person to start doing ten prostrations, adding one every week or two until he reaches fifty prostrations for instance.

Another father said, "the worshiper can prostrate once at the beginning of prayer, then at the end of each psalm. or at every word of prostration that is mentioned in the prayer.," but it is better if prostrations are combined together, either before prayer or right after prayer all at once; as the spiritual struggler feels great spiritual pleasure with it. St Isaac says, "Prostrate at the beginning of your prayer, and ask God with meekness and humility to grant you patience and control of thoughts in prayer."

---

[76] The paradise of the fathers

The average and appropriate number for an ordinary person living in the world is thirty or thirty-three prostrations; which should not be exceeded except for a few exceptions. As for monks, it exceeds that number but gradually; as the monk enters into a spiritual economy different with regard to the number of prostrations. Especially in certain seasons and situations, such as fasting and periods that require special spiritual struggle; where prostration is combined with other ascetic forms.

It is mentioned in the Philokalia about the number of prostrations as follows:[77] "with regard to the number of prostrations -metanoias- we know that according to the canon of the holy fathers, the number of prostrations must be three hundred, and you must perform them day and night within five days of each week, because we were asked to refrain from performing them on Saturdays and Sundays, and on some days and weeks that are decided by custom for other reasons. Nonetheless, some people perform more prostrations than this number, and others perform fewer prostrations. It is good for each person to perform the number of prostrations that are consistent with his strength and will, so you must also perform the number of prostrations that are truly proportional to your strength. Blessed is he who pushes himself to perform divine works. "The kingdom of heaven suffers violence, and the violent take it by force" (Matthew 11:12)."

Prostrations for the beginner can be divided into several groups. A first for thanksgiving and glorification, a second for repentance, a third is for praying for others, and a fourth can be dedicated to a specific matter.

---

[77] From the sayings of the saints Kalitos and Ignatius / The Philokalia - translation of Mikhail Tawfik - p. 259-260.

When are Prostrations Done?

The appropriate time for prostration is the early morning, either before prime hour prayer, or immediately after it, so that the worshiper gives God the first effort (physical strength) of the day and before using this effort in any other works or interests. This time is suitable for physical movement or activity on an empty stomach. However, there is no problem with distributing it over periods of the day - especially with large numbers - provided that it is not made immediately after eating, but rather after at least two hours have passed. But since prostration is an ascetic work, it is very appropriate to do it with fasting coupled with prayer. St. Isaac says, "A full stomach causes an extreme heaviness in the body, with loosening of the shoulders, which leads to neglect of the divine work and laziness to the work of the prostrations and the usual worship."[78]

As for those who spend the night in vigil in spiritual work (reading, meditating and praying), it will become appropriate for them to perform prostrations while they are in watch. They would pray one watch of the midnight prayer followed by a number of prostrations. Then they continue their work of reciting or praise, and afterwards they pray the second watch, followed by prostrations... and so on in the prayer. Saint Gregory says, "If a person fasts and stays up at night standing, singing psalms, kneeling and prostrating and cries and leaves his belongings. Isn't that struggle?" And he also said, "we must learn from those who have personally experienced the suffering and works of active virtue and practiced it; that is: abstinence fasting, bitter

---

[78] The Homilies of St. Isaac / Fr. Isaac Attala / p. 102

austerities, long night prayers, painful kneeling and the continuous standing without movement."[79]

Hegesippus, one of the scholars of the second century A.D., tells about St. James the Righteous (Just), Bishop of Jerusalem, that he used to make prostrations so much that the skin of his knees thickened and became like the knees of a camel.[80]

Times to refrain from prostrating

As for the times in which it is not accepted to perform prostrations as an ascetic behavior and an expression of contrition are; Saturdays, Sundays, the Lord's feasts, the period from the Nativity Feast to the Feast of Circumcision, the period from Nayrouz (beginning of Coptic Year) to the Feast of the Cross and Holy Pentecost following the Feast of Resurrection, for they are days of joy that are not appropriate for lamentation and contrition. As for the days in which we partake of the Holy communion, prostrations are also not permissible, unless the person is careful and performs them before the start of the Divine Liturgy. However, communion does not prevent one from worshiping in front of the altar of God, as well as the beginning of prayer in the inner room.

Also, patients who suffer from pain in the spine and the elderly (if their physical strength does not allow them to) are exempt from prostrations. That is because the body afflicted with disease or old age does not need to be burdened with prostrations as it carries a cross already.

---

[79] The Philokalia, p. 107
[80] The Dictionary of Church Fathers / Fr. Tadros Yacoub Malaty

Lastly, prostrations remove the weariness that comes from the devil and disperse bad whims, and return to the soul its vitality and to the body its strength.

"That at the name of Jesus every knee should bow, of those in heaven, and of those on earth, and of those under the earth, and *that* every tongue should confess that Jesus Christ *is* Lord, to the glory of God the Father" (Philippians 2: 10-11).

4

Habit Formation

Introduction

"But if anyone seems to be contentious, we have no such custom, nor do the churches of God" (1 Corinthians 11:16).

There is nothing more problematic than the formation of a bad habit, for it infiltrates into the depths of the person and blends with his emotions and his functions, and with time, it becomes an integral part of the personality, and an unsurmountable or at least difficult obstacle to overcome if one tries to free himself from it.

Saint Basil the Great says about the habit: (a persistent habit acquires all the strength of nature.)[81]

St Isaac adds saying; (Also, the manners and habits that were formed in man become like a second nature to him).[82]

---

[81] Philokala Vol. III
[82] Paradise of the Fathers

The danger lies in the fact that some habits may hinder the salvation of the souls, if the person does not have the discernment to set out what is good and what is not, or what is fitting and what is not.

"All things are lawful for me, but all things are not helpful. All things are lawful for me, but I will not be brought under the power of any" (1 Corinthians 6:12).

"All things are lawful for me, but not all things are helpful; all things are lawful for me, but not all things edify" (1 Corinthians 10:23).

How does a habit form?

A habit is formed subconsciously in a person. While one is leading his life normally, with time he finds himself bound to certain habits and terms. Initially it happens with one's consent and approval, and slowly these habits become rooted in personality and in emotions occupying the mind and the will. For example, when someone goes through a surgery, he takes medication like morphine to alleviate the pain, but if he takes it excessively it will become a habit that the person cannot live without.

This is called addiction, where chemical changes occur to the blood cells which requires a long term plan to treat, and if done wrong or quickly it may have severe consequences that may lead to death.

A habit also may form through imitating others. For example, when kids watch their Sunday School teacher praying, they mimic him, consequently this turns into a habit that could stay with them for the rest of their lives. Same goes for the way they behave, the way they talk, etc.

Now we can see that many of our habits that have become a part of our personality, can be traced back to imitation at early age.

Other reasons for habit formation, is the link between a time and an act or between a person and an act, so when the time comes or the person arrives to a place a certain behavior occurs. For example, when certain people wake up, they go in a carefully measured manner to the kitchen to prepare the morning coffee. They fill water, adding cream and sugar to their cups, all in precisely calculated quantities. As soon as it is done, they lift it, pour it in the cup, sit in a chair, sip it perhaps without pleasure, and without even needing coffee at all. Rather, they may leave it to cool without finishing it, all of this is done in a precise and dull way, repeating daily the same number of steps. the same number of movements and the same routine

What is a habit

A businessman told me once, that he always keeps a cup of coffee on his desk, whether filled or not. He absolutely has to have that cup in front of him and it doesn't matter if he drinks it or not and without it he becomes edgy. Accordingly, he links between it and his work, associating it with clear mind, relieve from headaches, and accomplishing tasks. This is the habit.

We can say the same about smoking. Some people cannot fall asleep or leave their beds before smoking, or even drink a cup of tea without a cigarette... etc. Some ladies also won't leave home before spending hours in front of their mirrors, to the point that make-up becomes a part of them and without it they become completely different. Here we see how bad habits become bound to the behavior.

Perhaps the most significant reason that contribute to the habit formation is the way parents raise their children. For example, if a mother teaches her child to pray every night before bed, when the child grows up will never go to bed before praying. Same goes for other habits like making their beds, brushing their teeth...etc. I know of a doctor who told me about one of his colleagues who wouldn't take even a quick nap before kneeling and praying. For sure he learned this from his childhood.

Thus, we find that whoever is accustomed to have his room neat and tidy will not accept it to be messy, or will not leave home without looking presentable. Also who was taught from young age to be grateful and polite with others doesn't tend to be otherwise.[83]

It is said that a child is psychologically formed at the age of seven (others say at the age of four), that is when the basic personality structure is established. Anything after that, is just minimal additions. It is also said that the conscious is formed between the ages of four and eight, and that whatever was subconsciously registered as morally right or wrong will be challenging to alter. Therefore, there is a great responsibility on parents and guardians to take heed to what kind of habits they are leaving their children with.

The monastic life is not different, where elders and spiritual fathers instill in young monks monastic and ascetic principles and habits. I remember that the new monastics from their first day were taught to use monastic vocabulary instead of the regular worldly talk, (i.e. I have sinned in place of sorry, God reward you instead of thank you, peace and grace in place of good morning...etc.) They are also taught how to

---

[83] Parents should consider applying this without overriding their children's personality.

interact with their elders, how to talk, how to behave in their cell and how to stay longer times in it which could be challenging in the beginning but when the habit settles in it becomes the sweetest practice in their life.

The habit may also form from a systematic repetition, and one must be watchful, and he must break this repetition, otherwise he will be enslaved to the habit. Saint Isaac said, "Do not let a habit take root in you and your mind will stay clear."[84]

The following two stories explain how an ingrained habit becomes a nature:

(1) In the palace: a kings asked his minister if politeness prevails over nature or the other way around, and the minister said, of course, nature since it is the origin. The king challenged the minister and brought some cats each holding a candle, which stunned the minister, who asked for time to think about this. The next day, the minister brought a mouse and once the cats saw it, they threw the candles and start chasing the mouse, to the point that they almost burnt the palace down, which proved the minister's point. As the poet says: "If he wants to be polite, his nature will attract him to the ancient era."[85]

(2) The little eagle: It was told that a farmer found a baby eagle, so he took it and placed among chicken and ducks. As the young eagle was growing eating the same food as chicken and ducks. When his wings got stronger, the farmer took it and went on a high mountain. He yelled;" you're an eagle your place is not among chicken", and he pitched the eagle up high. The young eagle flew away until it disappeared.

---

[84] Paradise of the Fathers
[85] This story was published in Coptic by Erian Farag in Ein Shams magazine, year 1 p.93

The significance of habits

The habit, when rooted in a person, turns into a feature that shapes and contributes to the formation of the personality. It lies beneath the main qualities of that person. As St Isaac said, "Be more attentive to habits than to your enemies, that whoever grows a habit, is like who adds gasoline to fire, if you do not answer to your habit, it gets weaker, and if you do, it will get stronger than before."[86] So the chatty, the gossipy, and the gluttonous, are people who have formed such habits, while not getting the proper direction from others, whether at home, in church, or from society. Here comes the importance of sincere advice from others towards what they see of bad habits. Thus the habit contributes to the formation of the person. St Isaac said, "Habits boost pains, and works establish virtue."[87]

Another thing, is the fact that it could deprive a person from doing good. For example, smoking prevents a person from partaking of the communion if he can't abstain for the required period, or if he can't fast in general. Also the habit of not waking up early may prevent the person from taking communion, therefore bad habits will prevent spiritual growth.

A person may lose his credibility in society because of his bad habits which cannot be tolerated by others. He also may lose his job, or not even get one because of them. Worse, it may even lead to sins. Fr. Maximus the confessor said, "One may sin by the force of habit, while another may sin because of an impulsive passion. The latter, did not intentionally sin, while the first thought of sin before committing it."[88]

---

[86] Paradise of the Fathers
[87] Paradise of the Fathers
[88] Philokalia vol.II on love

Habits may cause health issues, such as masturbation, consuming alcohol and other habits. The body is a talent that we have to take care of as St. Paul said "For no one ever hated his own flesh, but nourishes and cherishes it, just as the Lord does the church." (Ephesians 5:29), and thus a person may perish because of his rooted bad habits, which affect his destiny. Fr John of Damascus said "Attachment to material matters generates lust and content in the person who is under this bond, which causes lack of interest to spiritual matters, and if these small habits became dominant, this person becomes unguidable since he is under the bond of these hidden habits until God intervenes and set him free."[89]

A Chinese proverb says:

> Sow a thought, you reap a word
>
> Sow a word, you will reap a deed
>
> Sow a deed, you will reap a habit
>
> Sow a habit, you reap a virtue
>
> Sow a virtue, you reap eternity

St Arsenious says: (Initiate to uproot the small weed of slacking, or else it will take root and become big forest).

And Fr Peter of Damascus said: "The habit, if established, derives its strength from nature, and if it is not nourished, it weakens and fades away, and a habit, whether it is good or bad, is nourished by time as fire nourished by fuel. That is why we must seek good and do it with all our ability so that the habit will form, and then it becomes nature. This is how saints gained great things through the little things."[90] He also said,

---

[89] Philokalia vol II
[90] Philokalia vol. III

"God provides good things to his children and He will not forsake them because of their weak faith, bad intention, or bad habit. And if God blessed a man with the light of knowledge, he would strive to destroy the bad habit, and when he decides to do so, the Grace of God will work within him. The Lord said few who are saved (Luke 13:23, 24). Perspectives seem sweet, but in reality, they are bitter. The wounded dog licks his wound to find comfort, however he does not know that he licks his own blood. The same goes for someone who eats so much not knowing the harm he is inflicting upon himself.

Everyone under the bondage of any habit, can undoubtedly repent, but habit attracts him backwards, and that is why the Lord says in (Matthew 11:12) "the kingdom of heaven suffers violence", not by normal means, but by overcoming the habit and lusts. Because if the Kingdom is taken by normal means, no one will be able to enter it. So the habit works its way slowly either toward evil or virtue. If it weren't so, we wouldn't have seen repentant sinners who walked the long way between sin and virtue, as when the habit is defeated repentance triumphs."[91]

It was said that a philosopher wanted to examine whether education and practice could change the intrinsic nature and habits, so he brought a pig bathed it, put a golden collar around its neck, and clothed it with very expensive clothing, then he walked with it on a nice street, so it walked with him calmly and obediently, but as soon as it saw a swamp of shallow muddy water, it escaped to play in it. When the philosophers re-cleaned it, the pig repeated what it had done earlier. It is like the sinner who repents and keep going back to the same sin "A dog returns to his own vomit," and, "a sow, having washed, to her wallowing in the

---

[91] Philokalia vol. III

mire." (2 Peter 2:22). At that moment, grace becomes the only solution is to change the nature.

Examples of habits

As we mentioned before, the habit generates in a very simple way. And if one realizes how much it will cost him in the end, he would have paid more attention. A habit appears as a normal behavior, or as a pressing urge, or even as unintended mistake. St Isaac said: "Every habit, if you willingly abide to, will eventually become as a master to whom you are obliged to submit."[92]

Masturbation "Youthful Habit":

It was called a habit because it turns with time, despite the person's frustration with it, into an urge. This habit is transmitted through bad experiences of an unfaithful friend.

First time, it happened after a long and exhausting fight accompanied by bad feelings of guilt and impurity, cutting him from praying and reading the bible. Second time, the fight became weaker, and third time, there was no fight. Forth time, it happened after he desired it, and fifth time, it happened without any pleasure. Sixth time was without feelings. Now it is an indispensable habit, and when he thinks about its effect on moral, spiritual, psychological and physical levels trying to quit it, he finds a great deal of exertion that becomes a risk to his spiritual life.

---

[92] Paradise of the Fathers

An elder said, "There is nothing more difficult than a bad habit, because it needs a lot of time and toil to uproot. All people can toil but not everyone has enough time. For many were taken by death before they were able to finish their struggle. And God only knows how their judgment will be."[93]

Smoking:

How did a smoker start smoking? He was pushed to share a cigarette with others, but he rejected, so they made fun of him. First time he tried, he suffocated and coughed a lot and they laughed. The next time he did not cough. Another time, it became easier, then, it was him who asked for a cigarette. Later he started buying single smokes smoking in hiding. These singles developed into a whole pack. Now he is a big smoker who smokes in public as if he is doing a serious and important work. Now, for health and financial reasons he is trying to quit smoking, but he can't, and his sincere friends are trying in so many different ways to help, but in vain. Even doctors gave him alternatives, but he can't. Objections were made by the family of his future bride as smoking is a sign of a weak man who is captive to his habit. Yet he is still subdued and can't liberate himself

A recent French study, shows that the average lifespan of a nonsmoker is 69 years, while it is reduced to 60 years in the case of a smoker. And what was said about smoking, can be said about caffeine, drugs and stimulants, going to night clubs, bars, fashion shows, cinemas, theaters, and so on.

---

[93] Paradise of the Fathers

Do you know how idol worshipping started? King Solomon explains this in his book of Wisdom. A young man died, and his father loving him so much ordered a sculptor to fashion a statue of his son out of a piece of wood. The father treated the statue as if it were a living son of his, by feeding, clothing and kissing it. He continued to do so for many years, and then his children imitated him and it became a habit in that house. Thus, it became a god in the house, later every house had its own god! It is the habit that derives its strength from the person's love for it enslaving him till it becomes a god! (Refer to Wisdom, chapter 14)

It's also mentioned in second book of Kings about those who were brought by the king of Assyria to live in Samaria, that each of them worshipped the gods that they worshiped previously, and they were from five regions: Babylon, Cuth, Avite, Hamath, and, Sepharvit. "They feared the Lord, yet served their own gods—according to the rituals of the nations from among whom they were carried away." (2 Kings 17:33). The danger here lies in that although, they feared the Lord, the God of Israel, because of the beasts that attacked them, they, could not give up idolatry.

An elder said (He who is used to sin is like a dog accustomed to eat from the butcher's garbage, every time they kick it away, it keeps coming back till they kill it), this is how the habit leads to physical and moral death.

The magnitude of common habits:

There are also customs common to people, which were done during special circumstances and for a limited time. These customs gained the power of a law in society. For example, some people are used to prepare very lavish gatherings, even when they don't have enough resources to do so, for fear of despair, which is a naive idea, or disapproval from others, which shouldn't be taken in consideration.

Like what is done during feasts and celebrations when the festivities are bound to certain types of foods and desserts and other things, which came to be a heavy burden on families. Those families spend heavy budgets on these things, and some may actually borrow money to do that. In addition, the habits of buying new clothes during the holidays, which exhausts those who are unable to do so... etc. There are also the customs that accompany marriages and weddings which we need to stop and get rid of.

We need to learn not to associate the joy of feasts with some superficial aspects, such as food and clothing, but rather let it be joy from our salvation. Also from serving the poor and the needy, so that we may share with them the joy of the feast. Hence we move from the social dimension to the spiritual. It was mentioned in the Paradise of the fathers that one of the fathers was found working in his cell on the commemoration day of one of the martyrs. Another monk scolded him saying, is it permissible for you to work while we are celebrating? He replied, this martyr has incurred great sufferings for our Lord Jesus Christ, so should I not work a little for the sake of my salvation.

The previous generations witnessed many unfortunate customs during the Feast of Saints and martyrs (*mawled*), which made them lose their spiritual joy and their ascetic and redemptive content. This prompted the church to forbid these customs, as Pope Cyril V issued a decree preventing people from visiting tombs[94] and practicing such bad customs. The Church is still making more effort to educate the people

---

[94] Visiting tombs was linked to many pagan customs like deep grief and ritual meals, see Tobit 4:17

about how to celebrate holidays in a spiritual way. His Holiness Pope Shenouda III said that the celebration of holy occasions must be also carried out in a holy manner.

Some useful and positive habits:

St Isaac said, "The bonds of the soul are the habits, whether good or bad, that a person has become accustomed to."[95] This is how good habits can contribute to the salvation of the soul, and as we said before, good habits can start from early age like waking up early and praying before doing anything, gratitude, forgiveness, hospitality, understanding, encouraging others, love of the brethren, generosity, and politeness. This will build a spiritual personality stable and influential in church and in society. The Bible told us some of these habits, such as when Jesus used to go to the mountain to pray (Luke 22:39), His habit of teaching the flock (Mark 10:10) and the habit of the disciples going to pray by the river (Acts 16:13).

How do we get rid of a harmful habit?

There is a principle in ascetic life says that the best way to do this is to combat fire with fire!! And we said before that there is nothing impossible in Jesus Christ. A strong will with humility overshadowed by Divine Grace enable us to get rid of any bad habit. "I can do all things through Christ who strengthens me." (Philippians 4:13).

Fr Dorotheos the ascetic said: "Natural knowledge of virtues and opposite habits appear in two aspects. The first is theoretical knowledge, when a person thinks about them while he lacks experience,

---

[95] Paradise of the Fathers

but rather at times he may not be certain of what to utter. The other is practical in which knowledge is affirmed by experience, then it becomes clear, strong and sincere. In light of this, obstacles come to mind on the way of acquiring virtues, such as the genuine incline to habits, which resists virtue by nature. With time, the mind will be attached to the earthly. This is the same effect that the stimulated senses have on the mind."[96]

St Luchious said: "I was hungry and wanted to eat, and it was not time to eat yet, so I said to my stomach, die, because you asked for food now. I will cut off from you what I gave you in time."[97]

The matter, then, requires confronting the soul with its weaknesses, with the inner conviction of the necessity of combating the habit. Some habits may need to be stopped immediately, while others require gradual solution. For example, if you speak fast, you need to practice to read aloud in private, but if you smoke, you need to stop immediately. The person may not be satisfied with cutting it voluntarily, however, he will have to stop it when he gets old and sick. Someone said, "I am sixty years old, my craving for some foods, such as sweets did not decrease, but my ability to control myself increased.

Fr Dorotheos the ascetic said: "The soul, that is captured by certain habits, is capable of overcoming them. Before the habit existed, one was deceived by ignorance. So it is necessary for a person to turn to the true knowledge of the essence of life, and then strive for righteousness, disdaining all the worldly matters, being assured that all will vanish. For what are these things compared to our true purpose."[98]

---

[96] Philokalia vol II
[97] Paradise of the Fathers
[98] Philokalia vol II

A habit like eavesdropping needs to be stopped immediately, not gradual. St Nilus said, "What will we benefit if we remain attached to what we left behind, keeping worldly things in our mind, like Lot's wife who looked behind and turned to a pillar of salt, as an example of disobedience (Genesis 19:26). It represents the power of habit that pulls us backwards after we have tried to take a choice of asceticism."[99]

However, a habit of gluttony that leads to obesity, need to be treated gradually through a planned diet. St Isaac said, "If you train your stomach not to eat bread, it will not ask for meat." He also said: "The sword of virtue and vice is the alteration of habits, which are bonds to the soul, demanding consistently their needs. With ease they are acquired, and with difficulty they are removed."[100]

The body is set to adapt to what we decide. If the will is strong, the body can be controlled, and will be glorified in heaven. The stomach is like any organ in the body, it is ready to shrink and expand, according to the amount of food consumed, that is why the hermits' stomach is the same size of that of a child. When father Abdel-Messhi al-Habashi fell ill, he went to the doctor, who told him that his stomach had become like the stomach of a three-year-old child.

St Ologious told his disciple: "O son, get used to weaken your stomach by fasting, because it is like wineskins, the more you store in it the big it will get."[101]

It was told that Saint Moses the strong, when he entered the monastery, his food was the equivalent of a whole lamb. The fathers helped him in an amazing way. They brought him a large tree branch,

---

[99] Philokalia vol I
[100] Paradise of the Fathers
[101] Paradise of the Fathers

and they agreed with him to provide daily food equivalent to the weight of the branch. With time and after several years the branch became very dry, and its weight has decreased, which in turn caused the amount of food to be decreased. He was known to be one of the most austere ascetics in the wilderness.

Among the good habits that a monastic learns at the beginning of his monastic life is the Jesus prayer (Lord Jesus Christ have mercy on me a sinner) as he repeats it using a rosary. On the first day and for a period of several months, he completes the rosary (33 beads) once a day, then repeats it several times during the day, and then increases the number of times until it resonates with the movements of the breath, as he says "Lord Jesus Christ" when he inhales resembling accepting Jesus Christ, and says "have mercy on me a sinner" when he exhales resembling Jesus cleansing him from sin. This way the monk is taught the Jesus prayer through repetition, so that it would become a part of him. Having learnt this good habit, it sanctifies thought, time, and the senses.

A care giver described the last days of an elderly patient, who was eighty, and was bound to certain habits as if they were part of him. Once he got up from bed at 7 he went to the bathroom. At 8 he drank a cup of tea and smoked. He was captive to smoking more than his illnesses of pulmonic impairment, cardiac fault and shortness of breath. At 4 he sat on his porch, crossed his legs, smoked a cigarette, when he was finished he threw the cigarette butt away. He went in a coma and was in the ICU and what happened next was really astonishing. At 7 exactly he soiled himself. At 8 he moved his hand towards his mouth as if he was sipping a drink. At 4 he moved and bent his leg and his hand was moving back and forth to his mouth then he moved his hand as if he was throwing something away from him

We can quit bad habits by substituting them with good ones. Fr Deodoros says; "The road to virtue seems very hard to beginners in the spiritual life, that is for our nature inclines to the easy and wide road to lusts. But to those who are well on their way, the road to virtue seems easier, that is for the bad habits been replaced by other good ones and through grace they diminish. Thus The Lord, when He puts us on the road to salvation, says; "Because narrow is the gate and difficult is the way which leads to life, and there are few who find it" (Matthew 7:14). But to those who accepted His Teachings He says powerfully; "For my yoke is easy and my burden is light" (Matthew 11:30). So initially we should struggle with rigor as The Lord Jesus Christ said; "And from the days of John the Baptist until now the kingdom of heaven suffers violence, and the violent take it by force" (Matthew 11:12). When God sees our rigor, love and toil He will grant us will and joy for the sake of obedience."[102]

Fr Peter of Damascus said; "The long established habit gains power of nature, but if you don't submit to it; progressively it will lose power and diminish. Time feeds habits, whether good or bad ones, like fuel to fire. So as much as we can we should seed and practice what is good till it becomes a rooted habit. Through the overcoming of simple habits, saints made victory in great wars."[103]

Lastly good habits and routineness

We should take heed that repetition of a good habit leads to monotony and routineness, in turn we try to avoid practicing it. This, for example, happens when practicing the rites of the church. A rite is a motion form

[102] Philokalia vol I
[103] Philokalia vol III

for our belief and dogma, and every ritual movement has a theological and spiritual dimension. If we lose this dimension the liturgical rites will turn into systematic habits of movements, hence we lose the theological element, consequently its pleasantness and influence. Thus the bible says "sing unto Him with understanding." This is not all, but the rite has to be in accordance with the spirit of the holy bible. Christ rebuked scribes and Pharisees because they annihilated the commandment on account of their habits and rites; "Why do you also transgress the commandment of God because of your tradition?" (Matthew 15:3) ... "For laying aside the commandment of God, you hold the tradition of men ... All too well you rejected the commandment of God, that you may keep your tradition ... Making the word of God of no effect through your tradition which you have handed down" (Mark 7:8,9,13).

A good habit needs thoughtfulness, and the goal of it needs to be clear at all times. St Paul the apostle rebuked the converted Jews in his epistle to them saying; "Not forsaking the assembling of ourselves together, as is the manner of some, but exhorting on another, and so much the more as you see the Day" (Hebrews 10:25). Apparently these Hebrews maintained the outer shape while they lost the inner meaning.

We as well often keep the form of a worship or a habit, meanwhile we neglect the motive behind it. Thus many of the spiritual fathers recommend that the spiritual canon of a person can be reviewed and reformed periodically. This is to evade the outcome of a habit void of its perspective.

Another reason for changing the habits other than monotony, is the devil who keeps track of our habits and our attitude, and by doing so he knows more about our thoughts, personality, and our economy. One of the monks told me that he used to wash his hands after finishing his work and directly he used to start his prayers. He noticed that every day when he started his prayers, he found a hindrance like a call from outside or a sudden headache or remembering something that he had forgotten. So he recognized that the devil might have linked between the washing of hands and praying. Then he changed his routine; he would pray without washing his hands, or washing his hands and not praying, or even he would change his schedule altogether, till he was saved from this devilish scheme.

St Nilus the ascetic said; "Why did the ecclesiastic law orders one to not exit the church from the same gate he entered?[104] This is a symbol of leaving behind the doubts and the old habits and proceeding to a way leading to sainthood. We can't advance while we are still attached to our sins, as it is unfortunate that the power of old habits bounds us not letting us raise to the sublime state that was once ours. Habits alter behavior that becomes a second nature, that is very hard to amend or evade. This second nature could be shaken but can't move, could be pressured but it is dominant. After a great deal of struggle could be ultimately changed. We have to carry on towards our first love leaving behind our bad habits."[105]

In summary; habits generate from systematic repetition, either in young age or in negligence in older age. Uninterrupted watchfulness is required, for bad habits hinder the salvation of the soul, while good habits contribute to the spiritual growth.

"I can do all things through Christ who strengthen me"

(Philippians 4;13)

---

[104] An old tradition
[105] Philokalia vol I

5

Psalm 50: The Psalm of Repentance

Psalm 50 is one of the seven psalms of repentance (6, 32, 38, 51 (50), 102, 130, 143), and a guide for repentance. It enables one to pray with depth offering repentance, and to rejoice in its fruits, tasting its sweetness, while saying, "My heart rejoices with Your salvation," feeling engulfed with comfort and joy of heart. This psalm was prayed by David the prophet after realizing his dreadful state because of the transgression he had committed. This psalm, therefore, is very suitable to a person who feels defeated; it starts with asking for mercy and ends with asking for joy and fortification for the entire church.

The church prays this psalm in the beginning of all liturgical prayers, right after the thanksgiving prayer, whether in the book of hours, the mysteries, the liturgy of the water, or the matins of Covenant Thursday, asking for mercy and confessing our unworthiness. Perhaps, in the past, psalm 50 was prayed after every thanksgiving prayer, so that prayers consist of two elements: thanksgiving and repentance. The psalm starts with asking for mercy and confession of sin, and it ends with preaching God and offering praise in Zion.

It is striking how David did not fall into such a grave sin during the period of Saul's persecution, or while enduring hunger and thirst, or during the days of shepherding in the mountains, but instead, while he was resting on his throne! After he sinned, God sent Nathan the prophet to him to instruct him to the importance of repentance.

"Then the Lord sent Nathan to David. And he came to him, and said to him: 'There were two men in one city, one rich and the other poor. The rich man had exceedingly many flocks and herds. But the poor man had nothing, except one little ewe lamb which he had bought and nourished; and it grew up together with him and with his children. It ate of his own food and drank from his own cup and lay in his bosom; and it was like a daughter to him. And a traveler came to the rich man, who refused to take from his own flock and from his own herd to prepare one for the wayfaring man who had come to him; but he took the poor man's lamb and prepared it for the man who had come to him.' So David's anger was greatly aroused against the man, and he said to Nathan, 'As the Lord lives, the man who has done this shall surely die! And he shall restore fourfold for the lamb, because he did this thing and because he had no pity.' Then Nathan said to David, 'You are the man! Thus says the Lord God of Israel: "I anointed you king over Israel, and I delivered you from the hand of Saul. I gave you your master's house and your master's wives into your keeping, and gave you the house of Israel and Judah. And if that had been too little, I also would have given you much more! Why have you despised the commandment of the Lord, to do evil in His sight? You have killed Uriah the Hittite with the sword; you have taken his wife to be your wife, and have killed him with the sword of the people of Ammon. Now therefore, the sword shall never depart from your house, because you have despised Me, and have taken the wife of Uriah the Hittite to be your wife." Thus

79

says the Lord: "Behold, I will raise up adversity against you from your own house; and I will take your wives before your eyes and give them to your neighbor, and he shall lie with your wives in the sight of this sun. For you did it secretly, but I will do this thing before all Israel, before the sun."' So David said to Nathan, 'I have sinned against the Lord.' And Nathan said to David, 'The Lord also has put away your sin; you shall not die. However, because by this deed you have given great occasion to the enemies of the Lord to blaspheme, the child also who is born to you shall surely die.' Then Nathan departed to his house." (2Samuel 12:1-15)

Have mercy upon me, O God, according to Your great mercy; and according to the multitude of Your compassions:

The psalmist begins by asking for mercy based on God's abundance of mercy, saying, "Have mercy on me, O God, as we have witnessed mercy in You; have mercy on me according to Your great mercy and not according to my sins." Likewise, in the Divine Liturgy, as soon as the priest proclaims God's judgment, "He will give each one according to his deeds," we cry out imploringly, as one being tried in the court, pleading to the judge, "According to Your mercy and not according to our sins." The same priest, however, who announces the judgement of God, continues to ask on our behalf, as our defender (our intercessor-presbyter): "Deal with us according to Your goodness," which means give us according to Your compassion and not according to our worthiness. In the Great Fast, we pray to God, "I know You are compassionate and merciful." Also, Joel the prophet says, "So rend your heart, and not your garments; return to the Lord your God, for He is gracious and merciful slow to anger, and of great kindness; and He relents from doing harm." (Joel 2:13)

Blot out my iniquity, wash me thoroughly from my iniquity, and cleanse me from my sin:

Removing something is different than covering it–think of the difference between an eraser and a white-out corrector. The latter covers, while the former erases. Such is the case with the person who forgives temporarily, but does not forget, such that when the situation calls for it, he remembers everything. On the other hand, to blot out is different; it restores the nature to its former state, as if the person did not sin at all! "I, even I, am He who blots out your transgressions for My own sake; And I will not remember your sins. Put Me in remembrance; let us contend together; state your case, that you may be acquitted." (Isiah 43:25-26). Moreover, the expression of "washing" is encouraging and gives hope. The word "thoroughly" indicates that no matter how much the person is tainted with sin, it is possible to restore him to his original state; if the person falls numerous times, complete healing is still possible. The thorough washing refers to the hideousness of sin that needs an immense amount of God's love and forgiveness. Repentance, restores adulterers to virgins, as if they did not commit the sin, just like a robe is restored to its former state by washing. Also the word "thoroughly" paints to us the picture of reaching the utmost status of purity. "I have blotted out, like a thick cloud, your transgressions, and like a cloud, your sins. Return to Me, for I have redeemed you." (Isiah 44:22)

Note: David the prophet mentions three words that best describe his status: "Sin," "Iniquity," and "Transgression."

-   "Sin" is literally "missing the mark", which means what we ought to have done an act of goodness that we did not do.

- "Iniquity" is breaking the commandment, trespassing or going astray.

- "Transgression" is complaining or rebelling against God.

For I am conscious of my iniquity; and my sin is at all times before me:

David did not argue with Nathan the prophet, but bowed his head down, for he was "conscious of his iniquity!" Confession always needs honesty with oneself. How beautiful it is for a man to be honest with himself, saying: "I know that I am a sinner, many may compliment me, but deep within, I know that I am a sinner." Confessing sins and repenting, as the sacrament of the Church is named "Repentance and Confession"; some confess only, but they have not repented first. Thus, when David the prophet stood before God heart-broken beseeching mercy and forgiveness, he was offering an example of repentance that we ought to imitate before God to reconcile with Him, which is done even before standing before the priest.

I do not put my sins before my eyes in order to fall in despair or doubt in God's forgiveness, but to remember that I am weak and susceptible to falling, as well as to not put much trust in myself. Inclining and slipping into sin is before me. "My sin is at all times before me" reminds us of what St. Moses the Strong did when he carried the bag of sand on his back while sand was dropping from it. As if he was saying, "I came to judge someone, while ignoring my own sins, and instead of them being in front of me, I put them behind me." Likewise, the sins of some people are behind them, they do not see them.

Sometimes we sin and people do not see us; and sometimes they see us but do not realize that we have sinned. Since God, out of His love, covers us and does not expose us, we should not, however, ignore our sins, but we should judge ourselves, for if we remember our sins, God forgets them, and if we forget them, God remembers them. In the old days, St. Macarius the Great said to one of the monks, "Judge yourself my brother before they judge you, for judgment is to God alone." Our judgment of ourselves exempts us from God's judgment, even if others judge us.

It is astonishing how David did not point the blame to Bathsheba, and did not find himself any excuses, accusing her for stumbling him, but instead, was careful to repent, pleading for his sin to be forgiven. Likewise, confession is blaming and not excusing oneself.

Against You only I have sinned, and done evil before You:

This is the main reason why we should confess first before God in our inner room. The prodigal son said, "I have sinned against heaven and before you." God sees what we do in the hidden places even if the people do not. We ought to be rebuked from our consciences and apologize to God for we have broken His commandment. David had sinned against Bathsheba, Uriah her husband, his own family, the whole nation, and against himself, but more so, he had sinned against God. The expression "done evil before You" means that sadly I have sinned and was not embarrassed from You. This is just like when St. Pisarion questioned St. Taees if there was another hidden place where she sinned. She answered him, "If you fear people, no one will see us here, but if you fear God, know that He sees us everywhere." From here, he asked her, "So, why then do you live in sin, and cause many men to fall in perdition?" and that is how he led her to repentance.

Likewise, Joseph the righteous said, "How then can I do this great wickedness, and sin against God?" (Genesis 39:9). He felt that this sin would not be against Potiphar nor his wife, but against God Himself. Based on this thought, the fathers teach us that sin is a temporary disbelief, because if the sinner remembers that God sees him, he would be embarrassed and quit. The psalmist says, "They have not set God before them." (Psalm 54:3). Now, some think that because they didn't put others in harm ways, they will not be held accountable for their sins. Yet, man and all of his senses, members , and thoughts are God's and God entrusted man on all of it.

That You might be just in Your sayings, and might overcome when You are judged:

The prophet is saying: "if I argue with You, I would be proven wrong." In another place, he says: "Do not enter into judgment with Your servant, for in Your sight no one living is righteous." (Psalm 143:2). This means that it is a lost cause to try to object or justify myself before God. God said to Job: "Would you indeed annul My judgment? Would you condemn Me that you may be justified?" (Job 40:8). This means that when we stand before God, there should be no blames, no complaints, and no murmuring, but confession of sin and plea for mercy. Similarly, those who justify their sins before their father of confession, others, and themselves, add more sins to themselves instead of getting rid of their sins. The only righteous one is God; we all like sheep have gone astray, there is none who does good, no, not one, they have all turned aside; they have together become unprofitable.

When Napoleon Bonaparte issued a sentence of death against one of the soldiers for a grave crime, the soldier's mom met with him and pleaded that he forgives her son. Bonaparte responded, "your son is a criminal and he deserves to die." "Have mercy on him for he is my only child," the mother pleaded again, only to receive the response, "your son does not deserve mercy." At this point, she said to him, "If he deserved mercy, it would be considered justice not mercy!" Bonaparte marveled at her logic and let go of her son. If the earthly kings know how to offer mercy and respond to beseeching, how much more God!

For, behold, I was conceived in iniquities, and in sins my mother conceived me:

As humans, we have inherited the original sin, an inclination towards evil and a corrupted nature. That is why St. Paul says, "Therefore, just as through one man sin entered the world, and death through sin, and thus death spread to all men, because all sinned." (Romans 5:12) Pelagius' heresy, discussed in the council of Ephesus, was that we did not inherit the ancestral sin. The fathers of the church answered him that in this manner, he would be abolishing the dogma of redemption, since if humanity did not inherit the sentence of death, there would be no need for the incarnation of the Only Begotten Son and His death on the cross. David the prophet here does not allot the sin to Adam, but reaffirms the righteousness of God versus the disobedience of man. He rebukes himself that he was the one that was inclined to sin like his father Adam.

For, behold, You have loved the truth; You have manifested to me the hidden and unrevealed things of Your wisdom:

Another translation from Beirut says, "For, behold, You were pleased inwardly with the truth; in secret, You manifest wisdom to me." We cannot comprehend the depth of God, for who has known the mind of the Lord? Or who has become His counselor? However, God has revealed His love for us, "But God demonstrates His own love toward us, in that while we were still sinners, Christ died for us." (Romans 5:8). Your hidden wisdom is that You love me, accept my repentance, forgive me, and wish for my salvation, for You desire all men to be saved and to come to the knowledge of the truth. This is God's wisdom and economy.

You shall sprinkle me with Your hyssop, and I shall be purified. You shall wash me, and I shall be made whiter than snow:

Hyssop is a well-known plant that was used as medicine in ancient times. It was used as a fragrance and as a mouthwash, and when added to vinegar, it was used as a painkiller. Ritually, it was used for sprinkling the blood of the Passover lamb,[106] as well as in the purification water,[107] and in the purification of the leper.[108] However, purification from sin cannot be done except through the blood of Christ, "without shedding of blood there is no remission." (Hebrew 9:22). Even the forgiveness we receive now, we receive it from the perpetual sacrifice of Christ. We receive it from the abundance of forgiveness He left us in the mystery of repentance and confession, "If you forgive the sins of any, they are forgiven them." (John 20:23)

---

[106] Exodus 12:22
[107] Numbers 19:6, 18
[108] Leviticus 14:6

As for the phrase, "I shall be made whiter than snow," it means reaching the ultimate level of purity. The image of snow is used instead of water because water has no color, while snow is white and much brighter. As it is mentioned about the Lord's clothes during the Transfiguration incident, "His clothes became shining, exceedingly white, like snow, such as no launderer on earth can whiten them." (Mark 9:3)

What whitens our clothes is the Blood of Christ; it is written about those who are saved, "[He] washed their robes and made them white in the blood of the Lamb." (Revelation 7:14). Thus, we clothe the baptized child in white clothes with a red ribbon to point at the fact that he became whiter than snow, for he whitened his clothes in the Blood of Christ. "The blood of Jesus Christ His Son cleanses us from all sin." (1 John 1:7)

You shall make me to hear gladness and joy; the humbled bones shall rejoice:

The expression "the humbled bones" (or according to the Beirut's translation: the bones which You have humbled, rejoice) expresses our humiliation because of sin. Another meaning is the inward humility that resulted from feeling the transgression. Sin has worn out David's bones and crushed his inward man, as it does with anyone who sins.

As for the joy and rejoicing that David the prophet desires to hear are the words of forgiveness. God's words bring joy and comfort, as dew brings to a dry land—words such as, "Your faith has saved you. Go in peace;" (Luke 7:50). "I am willing; be cleansed;" (Matthew 8:3). "I who speak to you am He;" (John 4:26). "Young man, I say to you, arise;" (Luke 7:14), or "Lazarus, come forth!" (John 11:43). There were many people that had their eyes on the lips of Christ, "Only speak a word, and my servant will be healed;" (Matthew 8:8). His words are not only words of joy, but give healing and life. Likewise, we await, with much eagerness, the last phrase in the absolution that the priest prays on us, "May God absolve you." For the treasures of the whole world do not come close to the value of this phrase, its effects and its results. From here, the bones are fattened and rejoice. "Blessed is the man to whom the Lord does not impute iniquity, and in whose spirit there is no deceit." (Psalm 32:2)

Turn away Your face from my sins, and blot out all my iniquities:

"Turn it away from my sins," and not "turn this face, the face of light, away from me." For I persistently ask, "Do not hide Your face from me; Do not turn Your servant away in anger; You have been my help; Do not leave me nor forsake me, O God of my salvation." (Psalm 27:9)

For the sinner, his sin is before his eyes at all times, not forgetting that he is inclined to fall at any time. Whereas, for God, may He turn His face away from our sins, forgetting the matter completely.

As for the prayer, "Blot out all my iniquities," it differs from the prayer in verse 2, "Blot out my iniquity." In verse 2, the psalmist is asking God to blot out the intended sin in the psalm—adultery, while in this verse, he prays for all his iniquities and not one in particular. David knows that he did not fall in this sin only, hence he asks God for the forgiveness of all his sins and iniquities.

Create in me a clean heart, O God; and renew a right spirit in my inward parts:

If this heart has become polluted, diseased and hardened, such that there is no treatment, may You create a new one in me. You, O God, have promised to grant a fleshly heart in place of the stony heart, "Then I will give them one heart, and I will put a new spirit within them, and take the stony heart out of their flesh, and give them a heart of flesh." (Ezekiel 11:19)

The right spirit means the straightness of behavior or a "straight heart." In the Old testament, we read that the good kings did what was right "straight" in the eyes of the Lord. Even David himself, it is said, "Because David did what was right in the eyes of the Lord, and had not turned aside from anything that He commanded him all the days of his life, except in the matter of Uriah the Hittite." (1 Kings 15:5) Likewise, it is written about Asa, "Asa did what was right in the eyes of the Lord, as did his father David." (1 Kings 15:11)

We pray this daily in the third hour, when we remember the descend of the Holy Spirit on the disciples on the day of Pentecost, and we continue, saying:

Do not cast me away from Your face; and do not remove Your Holy Spirit from me:

Casting away from the face means total rejection for the person, even if he kneels, ignoring him, refusing his petition, and even refusing for that person to stand before Him. David himself, who accepted the mediation between him and his son Absalom to bring him back to Jerusalem, requested to not see him. "And the king said, 'Let him return to his own house, but do not let him see my face.' So Absalom returned to his own house, but did not see the king's face." (2 Samuel 14:24) Likewise, David prays, "Do not reject me, do not hide Your face from me; do not turn Your servant away in anger; You have been my help; do not leave me nor forsake me, O God of my salvation." (Psalm 27:9)

As for the Spirit, it is possible that He grieves and becomes quenched. It says, "Do not grieve the Holy Spirit of God," (Ephesians 4:30) and "Do not quench the Spirit," (1 Thessalonians 5:19) thus, it is possible that we ignore His rebuking. The Spirit, however, remains inside us, which is why we ask God to not remove Him from us. This was the case with Samson when he belittled his talent and forsook his vow. "And she said, 'The Philistines are upon you, Samson!' So he awoke from his sleep, and said, 'I will go out as before, at other times, and shake myself free!' But he did not know that the Lord had departed from him." (Judges 16:20).   Likewise, King Saul was punished with a similar outcome, "But the Spirit of the Lord departed from Saul, and a distressing spirit from the Lord troubled him." (1 Samuel 16:14)

Give me the joy of Your salvation, and uphold me with a directing spirit:

Free salvation is delightful, and so is salvation from sin. Some, however, are saved as through fire; [109] some are pained while struggling; some suffer while fasting; others weep and grieve when they repent, but ultimately, salvation is pleasant. If one is always doing things by force, one must examine this, as forcing should only be needed at the beginning. That is why in some translations, it says, "Restore to me the joy of my salvation," and elsewhere, it says, "But I have trusted in Your

---

[109] 1 Corinthians 3:15

mercy; my heart shall rejoice in Your salvation." (Psalm 13:5). Salvation is the beauty of Christianity and the source of our joy in this world!

Then I shall teach the transgressors Your ways; and the ungodly men shall turn to You:

When I taste your salvation, I cannot help but tell the others, "Oh, taste and see that the Lord is good!" (Psalm 34:8). There is no doubt that when David went through this experience, he was able to transfer it to others whose hearts had also been broken through sin and who had distanced themselves from God into despair. "I shall teach the transgressors" means, "I guide them to Your path," the path of forgiveness, acceptance, and forgetfulness of sin. Oh, how loving You are, O God! God has allowed those who fell into sin to become merciful to those who fall. We see this in the lives of St. Augustine, St. Moses the Strong, and many others. Also we read in the Paradise of the Fathers about that elder who failed to give hope to a sinner and lead him to despair, so another wise elder prayed to God to leave him to be tried in his old age with what he hadn't been tried with in his young age, in order to teach him to have compassion on sinners.

Deliver me from blood, O God, the God of my salvation, and my tongue shall rejoice in Your righteousness. O Lord, You shall open my lips, and my mouth shall declare Your praise:

In spite of his repentance and his joy with the salvation of the Lord, David had left his offspring the inheritance of the sword and adultery. We read, "Now therefore, the sword shall never depart from your house, because you have despised Me, and have taken the wife of Uriah the Hittite to be your wife." (2 Samuel 12:10). What David had done, Absalom and Amnon, his sons, and many of his grandchildren, did likewise. The wars and the murders continued, and the son that was born as a fruit of sin, died.

This shows that the consequences of sin can be passed on as inheritance, even after offering repentance; like consequences of addiction, gambling, bad habits, adultery, usury, murder, etc. Some sins have earthly punishments, even with repentance. "Blood" does not necessarily mean murder, but the responsibility for the perishing of people. For example, when God warned the slacking shepherd that He will ask for the blood of the flock from him, He did not mean that the flock's blood was shed, but that they perished. When we pray this part of the psalm, we ask to be saved from the responsibility of anyone that might perish because of us, whether through stumbling or negligence.

"My tongue shall rejoice in Your righteousness" means that my tongue rejoices when speaking about Your mercies, for Your justice is full of mercy. The psalmist finds joy in speaking of His justice, "And my tongue shall speak of Your righteousness and of Your praise all day long." (Psalm 35:28). Elsewhere, he says, "They shall utter the memory of Your great goodness, and shall sing of Your righteousness." (Psalm 145:7).

Lips are opened when the heart overflows with thanksgiving and joy. He who teaches my hands how to fight, teaches my lips how to praise; and He who reveals wonders to the eyes, is the same one that teaches prayer and praise. The tongue proclaims God's righteousness, as a witness to You before all.

God grants speech and wisdom to those who witness, as we saw during the times of persecution. He promised, "But when they deliver you up, do not worry about how or what you should speak. For it will be given to you in that hour what you should speak; for it is not you who speak, but the Spirit of your Father who speaks in you." (Matthew 10:19-20). "O Lord, open my lips" is the psalmist's way of saying, "I do not open my own lips, but let it be You who puts on my lips what needs to be said."

For if You desired sacrifice, I would have given it; You do not take pleasure in burnt offerings. The sacrifice of God is a broken spirit:

The greatest thing we can offer to God is a humbled heart. God Himself says, "For I desire mercy and not sacrifice, and the knowledge of God more than burnt offerings." (Hosea 6:6). More than once, God has declared that He had enough of burnt offerings, and instead, He desires the broken heart that is offered wholly to God willingly and happily, considered the greatest of all sacrifices. "'To what purpose is the multitude of your sacrifices to Me?'" says the Lord. 'I have had enough of burnt offerings of rams and the fat of fed cattle. I do not delight in the blood of bulls, or of lambs or goats.'" (Isaiah 1:11)

Picture someone standing in prayer with haughtiness like the Pharisee, or someone who puts money into God's treasury with pride of heart, or someone who serves without humility; this is not the sacrifice which God desires. Instead, God rejoices when we offer with meekness, regardless of what we offer.

A broken and humbled heart God shall not despise:

God loves the humble. It is the humble person who acquires God's kindness and forgiveness. A humble person's tears move God's

93

compassion, regardless of his sin, for his humility abolishes the walls of sin. The mercies of God would rain down upon him, for God gives grace to the humble. Even amongst ourselves, an apology from the heart receives acceptance, comfort and forgiveness. When we sin, we must stand before God with brokenness and say humbly that we have sinned, asking for forgiveness with a guilty and sorrowful heart. We shall stand just as the tax collector did when he said to himself: no matter what I say or how beautifully I put it, I will never be able to express how sorry I am before God. Therefore, he said with brokenness without daring to lift his eyes above, "God, be merciful to me a sinner." (Luke 18:13). He does not just see himself as one of the sinners, but rather, the only sinner, the chief sinner. Many others have humbled themselves before God, and we follow their example, such as: Hannah, Esther, Judith, Augustine's mother, the sinful woman, etc.

Do good, O Lord, in Your good pleasure to Zion (the Church); and let the walls of Jerusalem be built:

How much do we need this petition today while living in the midst of tribulation and persecution! How much do our churches and hearts need the stability of God's peace in them! May You fill our lands and houses with goodwill, and remove from them the long-lived gloominess and melancholy. As for the walls of Jerusalem, they are what fell because of doubt, disbelief, and estrangement from God. The walls are the support and the strength of the Church. Zion can also refer to the heart and Jerusalem to the person, just as Zion was the hill which the temple was built upon. Let the heart rejoice, and the walls of Jerusalem be well, that is, all its members and all its senses, and let Jerusalem, the person, be guarded by God.

Then they shall offer calves upon Your altar. Alleluia:

The continuity and consistency of the sacrifices in the tabernacle or the temple were a sign of God's approval and an indication of the stability of the nation. Sometimes, God allowed the sacrifices to discontinue, and we read in the book of Judith how the discontinuing of sacrifices brings the wrath of God. Judith told Holofernes, the chief of the Assyrian armies, that once the city runs out of animals, the sacrifices will stop, which will announce the wrath of God on the nation. In fact, the sacrifices had stopped multiple times in the days of David, Saul, during the exile, and the days of Antiochus Epiphanius. In another translation, the sacrifice refers to the sacrifice of praise, which is pleasing to God. Alleluia

This psalm is a joyful tiding: God forgives, accepts the sinners returning to Him, and accepts the burnt offerings:

From the depth of darkness, I cry out to You, so let me hear Your compassionate voice. From the mire of sin, I lift up my hands; as a child wallowing in his filth stretching out his dirty hands with spiteful transgressions to You, so stretch out Your hands to me, purify me and pull me out.

Hasten to me, for behold the devil is standing at the door of hades, baring his fangs, thirsty to devour me, and to lock me there. They ambush me, but You pave to me the path of salvation, "So the poor have hope, and injustice shuts her mouth." (Job 5:16)

My hope in You is the rock that I hold on to when the waves slap me; it is the ray of light that guides me to You. When I look at my sins, I tremble and fall in despair and depression, and when I come to You, do not turn Your face away from me. When I am indulged in sin, do not leave me, but rather pull me against my will, for I do not know what is beneficial to me. One of the saints that have tasted Your forgiveness said, "If You have mercy on the righteous only, it is not a wonder, but if You manifest Your strength in me, a sinner, this is truly wondrous!"

I have hope that You do not deal with me according to my sins, but according to Your mercy. Let go of my sins, for I know that the door is open as long as I remain in the flesh. Therefore, I hasten now while I am still alive, "Not that I have already attained, or am already perfected; but I press on, that I may lay hold of that for which Christ Jesus has also laid hold of me." (Philippians 3:12)

6

Redeeming the Time

"See then that you walk circumspectly, redeeming the time because the days are evil" (Ephesians 5:15-16). St Paul speaks to the Ephesian church warning them—in his ceaseless fatherly love—to awaken and be watchful that times are swift, and to care for their eternal life pointing them:

A- Watchfulness (Spiritual foresight)

B- Wisdom in conduct (Choosing the path, and spiritual advancement)

C- Circumspection (Faithfulness to the path, and life of solemnity)

D- Time redemption (Investing it fittingly)

E- How days are evil (Which require more watchfulness and alertness)

A - Watchfulness

Why are sheep so easy to stray away, losing their path and their shepherd, while cats, for example, do not? A lamb moves between a mound of grass and another without lifting its head, so in no time, it loses its path and its herd. A cat, on the other hand, lifts up its head and gives a quick look around while eating to scan its location, so it does not lose its way.

In that same manner, a struggler needs to review himself every now and then to see where he stands, so that if he has drifted away from his path and goal, he discovers this before it is too late. Otherwise, he will either despair and continue in the wrong path, or, only if he has hope, he will toil greatly to correct his path.

Man needs a still and a firm point outside his busy life, where he can stand to see the big picture, to examine his state, and to establish his position with God. The more a person drifts from God, the more God becomes far from him.

Simple view versus deep examination

The word "see", used by St. Paul in the above-mentioned verse, does not mean a simple quick look but rather deep observation and examination. In Coptic, there are two word to express seeing; one is "*soms*" which means "to look at", and the other is "*gosht*" which means "to behold" or "to closely observe."

In the Wednesday Theotokia refrain, we sing, "The Father looked ("gosht") from heaven and found no one like you," meaning that God the Father searched and examined until He found that St Mary, who was "the worthiest" from whom His Son was to take flesh.

Consequently, when St Paul used the word "see", he means to watch closely and persistently. When the Lord asked His prophet Jeremiah to look for a righteous person in Jerusalem that He might save His people from exile for his sake, He said to him; "Run to and from through the streets of Jerusalem; See now and know and seek" (Jeremiah 5:1).

See… Look into the matter

"See" here means "look into the matter" to make a decision. As we read in the trial of our Lord Christ, Pontius Pilate said to the Jews, "I am innocent of the blood of this just Person. You see to it" (Matthew 27:24). Pilate was asking the Jews to study, examine, and make a decision. Pilate did not mean to use their eyes and physically look, but rather to examine the situation and come to a decision. The Jews, however, could not see, as the Lord Jesus told them, "Having eye, do you not see?" (Mark 8:18). The Jews said the same thing to Judas when he wanted to return the silver with which he gave up His Master. They said to him, "What is that to us? You see to it" (Matthew 27:4).

There, then, is a difference between sight and examination, just as there is a difference between listening versus understanding, and obeying. When a father tells his son to listen to him, he actually means to comprehend and obey him. When Solomon the wise says, "The wise man's eyes are in his head" (Ecclesiastes 2:14), he means that the wise is a watchful and vigilant person who can examine things, while the fool walks in darkness.

Foresight

Some people have their eyes and target at their feet, while others have them a few meters away, and even fewer have their targets on the far horizon... on eternity!

One of the marvels of the monastic life is that monastics, for their long life in the desert and wilderness, have that foresight to focus on the joyful eternity. They do not care for the worldly things which they can see close by.

St Paul says, "while we do not look at the things which are seen, but at the things which are not seen. For the things which are seen are temporary, but the things which are not seen are eternal" (2 Corinthians 4:18).

The watchful person examines his reality and comprehends, resolves, and relates it to his journey to Christ who is the Way and the Goal. Our ultimate goal is to reach heavenly eternal life, so we eagerly look forward for it.

Guidance

If one cannot see well and discern, as St Paul says in Romans 3:18 and Philippians 1:10, one must seek help from their spiritual guide. Submit to him and see with his eyes instead, as one who uses a lens for better vision, as often, things appear different from their reality. "There is a way that seems right to man, but its end is the way of death" (Proverbs 14:12). The wise guide sees what his disciple cannot.

In actuality, seeking guidance, if not built on man's discerning will and his intent on the necessity of change, will be futile.

Seeing and aiming

Seeing and determining our goal is the base for choosing the path to follow. Aiming correctly will help us hit the target. Interestingly, the word "sin" in Greek means "failing to hit the target."

Sin deviates us from the purpose for which God created us, that is to live joyfully in His company. Balaam, son of Beor, said about Jesus Christ; "The utterance of the man whose eyes are opened... with eyes wide open... I see Him, but now, I behold Him but not near" (Numbers 24:3, 15-17).

The circumcised (sanctified) eye

Circumcision was a symbol for the new life obtained in baptism. As the Lord points out to His people in the Old Testament, true circumcision is that of the heart, of the mind, and of the senses. "And The Lord your God will circumcise your heart and the heart of your descendants, to love The Lord your God..." (Deuteronomy 30:6).

St Paul also says, "And circumcision is that of the heart, in The Spirit, not in the letter, whose praise is not from men but from God" (Romans 2:29).

Thus, spiritual circumcision is sanctifying our members and consecrating them to God alone, so that the circumcised heart is Christ's, the circumcised ear listens and obeys, the circumcised hand extends with goodness, the circumcised leg follows righteousness, and the circumcised eye sees well and enjoys enlightenment, i.e., sees the truth and experiences it.

When St Paul says in the beginning of the verse, "See then that you walk", he means to examine, look into, watch, and decide how you will walk circumspectly, since God offered redemption for mankind, and He shed His precious blood for us.

Yet salvation of man is a bilateral work between God and man. God initiated by His coming down to save that which had perished, and now man's role is to accept this salvation. St Augustine says, "God who created you without your will wills not to save you without your will." Also the Lord speaks by His prophet Isaiah saying, "Look to me and be saved" (Isaiah 45:22).

Now we must look towards God with our hearts and eyes and see how to walk circumspectly.

B - Wisdom in Conduct

We discussed so far about how to see the way and the path of our lives, and we mentioned that the word "see" does not refer to the simple act of seeing but rather it means to examine closely and to review. Now we will talk about conduct.

To whom does St. Paul write?

St. Paul wrote his epistle to the Ephesians, from which we find our verse of focus. The Holy Spirit directed his words to a people who lived far away from the light of the Gospel, lost in the darkness of sin and perdition. The city was fond of worshipping the idol goddess Diana and its impressive temple was one of the Seven Wonders of the World to which millions of idol worshippers flocked every year. It was such that the trade of sculptures flourished, as we see in Acts 19:21-40, and along with that, sin increased because of the lavish life of its people. Moreover, thieves and criminals took refuge in the city living in a village nearby the temple. St. Paul warned them saying, "For you were once darkness, but now you are light in The Lord. Walk as children of light" (Ephesians 5:8.)

Choosing the path

If someone does not choose his path, the path of perdition will choose him, because whoever does not strive to raise himself, gravity will inevitably bring him down. It is just like a person driving his car and controlling the steering wheel. If he loses control, he will become horrified of what is to come.

St Paul fervently pleads his readers saying, "This I say, therefore, and testify in The Lord, that you should no longer walk as the rest of the gentiles walk, in the futility of their mind" (Ephesians 4:17).

In the first hour of Agpeya, the church assigned a passage from the same epistle to the Ephesians, setting the standard for our conduct throughout the day. "I, therefore, the prisoner of The Lord, beseech you to walk worthy of the calling with which you were called", and we are called Christians... after Our Lord Jesus Christ... and thus, we must to walk in righteousness. "He who says he abides in Him ought himself also to walk just as He walked" (1 John 2:6).

Walking watchfully

Just as a captain of a ship sails safely amongst rocks and mines, assisted by specific devices, as well as his experience and responsiveness, or just as a man who treads a thorny land should be watchful, not only when hazard is expected but also when it is least expected, we also should be watchful because the devil is deceitful and illusive. We must scan our surroundings to ensure we are walking straight and not deviating even in the slightest. This is where the role of the spiritual guide comes in. As in a battlefield, the soldier is saved if he obeys his commander who can see the bigger picture.

Life is a journey. It could either be a journey of charity, inspiration, and overwhelming joy along the road, or it could be a confusing maze. Some choose the narrow road to reach their destination quickly, and others choose the wide and easy road, but they easily go astray. "Because narrow is the gate and difficult is the way which leads to life, and there are few who find it" (Matthew 7:14).

Walking with perseverance

There are some who, in the midst of many hardships and opposing powers, walked having their trust in God and with self-confidence, they were able to make these sufferings recede and diminish before them. Thus says the Bible, "Who are you, O great mountain? Before Zerubbabel you shall become a plain" (Zechariah 4:7).

Satan recedes and withdraws before the strong, while he dares to insolently attack the weak who stay heedless before him. It is just as a wild beast who will chase you if you run from it, and will run from you if you chase it.

Whoever walks according to God's will with a strong heart does not fear what he will face, while the lazy stay faint-hearted in heedlessness. "The lazy man says, there is a lion in the road, a fierce lion is in the streets" (Proverbs 26:13). The Preacher also says, "He who observes the wind will not sow, and he who regards the cloud will not reap" (Ecclesiastes 11:4).

The wretched one piles rocks on the road blocking it and then stands helplessly baffled before it, whereas the hopeful walks in the company of Christ–the Way–who provides the expenses of the journey. It is as the prophet Isaiah said, "The way of the just is uprightness, O most Upright, You weigh the path of the just" (Isaiah 26:7). The warrior, on the other hand, when he comes upon a stumbling rock on the way, picks it up and puts it aside so he can carry on along the road. Even if he falls– whether due to negligence or due to the intensity of the war–he picks himself back up, eager to continue his journey. A saint once said, "Man can have a new beginning everyday if he is a fighter." Whoever contently and wisely chooses his path from the start does not question his choice, and when doubts attack him, he surely knows that it is a war that will shortly end.

I press on that I may lay hold

"But I press on, that I may lay hold of that for which Christ Jesus has also laid hold of me" (Philippians 3:12). Here, St. Paul does not speak of merely pressing on, but rather pressing on *fervently*. He uses this metaphor from the sport of running a present day marathon. Competitors strive vigorously to win the prize, likewise, the spiritual struggler will need to strive fervently, fixing his eyes on the prize, which is eternal life. Remember the runner who cheated his competitor by throwing golden coins in his track, distracting him from the race every time he stopped to pick them up and ultimately lost the race altogether. Similarly, a soldier fighting in a war must focus on his targets and not be distracted by whatever spoils he sees. A true struggler believes that God awaits him in His eternity since before time.

But who is the way?

Christianity in the beginning was called the Way, because it was a way of conduct and a way for virtue (Acts 19:9, 23). Christ is the Way and the How, the Goal and the Means. We reach God through God Himself. "As you therefore have received Christ Jesus the Lord, so walk in Him" (Colossians 2:6).

Walk versus conduct

No doubt that when a person walks in his life, he determines and makes the outcome of his conduct. The Bible says, "Remember those who rule over you, who have spoken the word of God to you, whose faith follow, considering the outcome of their conduct" (Hebrews 13:7). We have innumerable saints who lived in solemnity, meekness and strong unshakeable faith, and formed a great cloud of witnesses surrounding us (Hebrews 12:1). These saints became our guides along the way. "If you do not know O fairest among women, Follow the footsteps of the flock" (Song of songs 1:8)

Some started their spiritual life solemnly, but soon fell in apathy. They may have trusted themselves more than they should and in turn, their resilience weakened and they became lukewarm. Endurance and perseverance is then very important for success.

The Thrice Blessed Pope Shenouda III said to those struggling in the spiritual way, "Run with all your power, and if you cannot, walk hurriedly, and if you cannot, walk steadily, and if you cannot, crawl, and if you do not find the power even for that, then standstill, but take heed not to go backwards." Once again, "See how you walk circumspectly."

C - Circumspection

A watchful person needs to examine himself from time to time, to ensure that his conduct and his goal is towards God. The more watchful he is, the more often he will do this, to the extent that it may even become a daily duty to the highly spiritual. This is when a person stands still to examine, judge, and review himself in order to correct himself and observe any deviation that occurred along the way.

St. Paul, in his epistle to the Ephesians, talks about the hard life that believers lived there, where sin abound in all its aspects and was overwhelmingly dominant. "And because lawlessness will abound, the love of many will grow cold" (Matthew 24:12). With time, some people even lose the ability to separate between good and evil.

This is when imitating and mimicking one's surrounding will increase sin, due to the distortion of concepts and the confused view of sin. Then, sin transforms into habit and consequently habit becomes a normal undetected behavior.

As a result, St. Paul warns them not to walk as fools driven by every wind looking only at their feet, entirely without their will, but rather to walk as wise men seeking enlightenment and wisdom from God, that they may approve the things that are excellent (Romans 2:18 and Philippians 1:10). That way, they do not belong to this world filled with evil and temptations, but they belong to heaven for which they long and where they put their utmost hope, where they will live with the Lord in His kingdom.

Virtues and pseudo-virtues

You may have heard before of the term "pseudo-virtue." It means that a person can be misled by a behavior thinking it is a virtue but in truth it is sin and a deviation. Take for example fake humility versus true humility, where the motive of the former is pride and pursuing vain praise from others, while the latter is a virtue pursued by someone who feels his weakness and feels the need for God's help and the prayers of others.

Philosophers define virtue as a mid-point between two opposites; extremeness and indifference. Generosity, for example, is a mid-point between lavishness (extremeness) and stinginess (indifference), courage is a mid-point between careless risk-taking and cowardliness, etc. There is then a big difference between asceticism and scarcity, fasting and loss of appetite, true humility and weak personality, being merry and ridiculing others, simplicity and gullibility, strong personality and pride, calmness and reclusiveness, being vigilant and sleeplessness, sensibility and sensitivity, a researcher and a teacher, a pastor and an instructor, a virgin and a bachelor, and sight and foresight.

Similarly, the difference between circumspection and obsession needs discernment. A circumspect person is solemn, faithful, and straightforward; he walks watchfully and wisely. A compulsive obsessive person, on the other hand, exaggerates the simplest matters, giving them more significance than they really are, his compulsion and obsessiveness may reach the point of psychological disorder, even to the point of vulnerability and wickedness.

A watchful person is solemn but not immoderate, kind but not indulgent, sincere in his kindness and kind in his sincerity. He is an icon of our sweet Christ, who is just in His love and loves in His justice. An obsessive person, however, is doubtful, suffers an abnormality in his personality, and runs even when no one is chasing him.

We read about one of the desert fathers who had to pay a visit to a sick elder in a day of the great lent. There, they offered him and his disciple food, so they ate. On their way back, the disciple saw water, so when he went to drink from it, the father stopped him kindly because it was a fasting day. When the disciple reminded him that they had just ate, the enlightened father answered, "We ate for brotherly love and now we do not break our canon." Watch how this saint behaved circumspectly without exaggeration.

The little foxes

We have heard and read of the little foxes. "Catch us the foxes, the little foxes that spoil the vines" (Song of Songs 2:15). While wolves go for the watermelons, they, awaiting near the fields and attacking at night, spoil the crops. Foxes go for the vines. They too await near the fields to attack at night to get an easy delicious meal. The alert vinedresser diligently checks the fence to cover any gaps and draws close its poles in order to stop the big foxes from entering the vine. In turn, the big foxes push their little ones between the poles to get them food, and these little ones spoil even more crops than they eat as they lack experience. These little foxes manage to hide easily when they feel danger, making it much harder for the vinedresser to catch them. This happens daily, and eventually the little ones live within the vine, where they grow and mate and reproduce more little foxes, and with time, these little foxes create a big problem.

Some think that spoiling the vine is a big job for a little creature running within it, so they do not give real attention to these little foxes, thinking they can get rid of them whenever they want. They cannot fathom how such little creatures could be a threat to a vast vine, but, indeed, how these can spoil many acres of grapes!

These little foxes resemble the small sins which hide behind the great virtues, the little foxes that man neglects, like a small lie, a cigarette, a website–out of curiosity, the hurried prayer–one time because of lack of time and another because of fatigue, and in the end all of this becomes a clear pattern. Waking up late, cutting liturgy attendance and so on. No doubt negligence leads to sin. It is like a derailed train that needs much more effort to be put back on its tracks.

True circumspection is self-control

It is easy to control and lead others, but the true test is self-control. The true struggler is tough on himself while easy on others. He does not pity himself but is compassionate to the weaknesses of others. He judges and rebukes himself but find excuses for others. He is circumspect in his spiritual canon, working with his spiritual father to move him from one level to another, doing exactly as he is directed. The true spiritual struggler can manage his time wisely.

He is solemn towards his school, his family, his society, and God. He considers his studies as a talent, a spiritual and moral obligation. In his conduct, he knows very well that he is an image of God. People see Christ through him. His words are seasoned with The Holy Spirit. He knows how to differentiate between the virtue of kindness and inappropriate mockery. There is a guard on his mouth, as well as a strong guard on all his senses. This is important as the senses gather and the mind stores and reacts, and as it enters the heart, this is how sin fulfills its willing path. This is why the prudent and watchful shut the doors of their senses so they do not lay the road for sin.

Watchfulness keeps your treasure without harm, leaving no room, due to negligence, for your treasure to be stolen or your spiritual sanity to leave you. Let solemnity, prudence and circumspection be according to God's will.

Moreover, circumspection does not mean putting on long faces and hard attitudes. It is not harsh orders nor austerity without discernment. This is why a spiritual father has an important role. Pray and ask unceasingly that God may grant you circumspection and wisdom so you may redeem the time.

D - Time redemption

St. Paul wrote this epistle while incarcerated in Rome. There, he fulfilled his worship as well as his pastoral work. Regarding these times, he says, "In journeys often, in perils of waters, in perils of robbers, in perils of my own countrymen, in perils of the gentiles, in perils in the city, in perils in the wilderness, in perils in the sea, in perils among false brethren" (2 Corinthians 11:26). Although he was a prisoner, he managed to add to the church three Christians everyday—the soldiers who guarded him over three shifts! Having spent eight hours with St.

Paul, the pagan soldier converted to Christianity. This is how St. Paul lives what he urges his reader, which is to redeem the time.

The value of time

The word "time" here does not mean the passing of minutes and days (Kronos), but rather the appointed time (Kairos) or the opportunity given to us by God. "Therefore, as we have opportunity, let us do good to all" (Galatians 6:10). Here, he means to acquire the opportunity and exchange it. The Greek verb "*ex-agorazw*" means to buy, as we read in Galatians 3:13 that Christ redeemed (i.e. "acquired") us from the curse of the law. The prefix "ex" gives the word a greater meaning and a much more powerful significance. The verb "*agorazw*" was used to express Christ's liberation to the believers—the Jewish descendants—from the curse of the law. He became under the curse of the law... "to redeem those who were under the law" (Galatians 4:5).

Redemption in essence means to transform the corrupted to uncorrupted, evil to righteousness, death sentence to liberation, and darkness to light. The price for this was suffering, crucifixion, and death. On the other side, man strives to transform the earthly temporal time to everlasting eternal time through his struggle, toil, vigilance, and unceasing charitable works. When he offers his sweat, blood, and tears, he exchanges the corruptible with the incorruptible, the temporal with the eternal, and the earthly with the heavenly. Some people try to redeem their eternity with their present, yet others—lacking wisdom—give away their eternity by holding on to the futility of the present. As the latter lost their trade, the former profited wisely...

...But how to find time...

The difference between the two is not that the first finds enough time to strive and achieve while the second does not. No, in fact the difference is that one multi-tasks and manages his time while the other does not. The first manages several entities simultaneously and works day and night, while the other passes his time leisurely in front of screens or in unnecessary social gatherings. If we do a simple review at the end of the day to compare our achievements with respect to time, we will find that hours went by without any fruits.

I imagine that God grants us every morning a "daily allowance" of twenty-four hours to accomplish what we could not finish the day before.

Moreover, the desert fathers used to read and pray while working, and they did not make work or meals a time-designated activity. Though they strived to accomplish several tasks at the same time (with prayer being the common factor with any other activity), they stopped frequently to examine their deeds.

We read about St Poemen who, while was painting his cell with his brother, stopped and wondered saying, "What if Christ comes now? Would He find us praying or doing such work?" Promptly, they left their work and went into their cells.

Sleep and time redemption

Furthermore, the desert fathers were very scarce with their sleep, to the extent that the word "sleep" is not preferred in the monastic vocabulary. Instead, monastics use the word rest, rather than sleep, as it is not appropriate indulge in sleepiness.

I wonder how some oversleep. In fact, the average person spends a third of his life asleep, so a thirty-year-old had slept for nearly ten years! Sleep can be seen as "a minor death" because one stays out of the circle of reaction with life and society. Death was referred to as sleep by our Lord Jesus when He said, "Our friend Lazarus sleeps but I go that I may wake him up" (John 11:11). Whoever is occupied with a great endeavor cannot oversleep!

Truly, a man's age is calculated by how much of his time he spends in labor, vigils, toil, doing good deeds, and generating fruit. The saints say, "One can accomplish in one hour what another cannot do in years if the first has vigorous intent while the second is negligent." I remember once asking an elder monk about the number of years he spent in the monastery, to which he answered me saying, "thirty years." When I commended him on this, he added, "but it is thirty times zero!" In humility, this elder monk felt that he did not accomplish anything worthy of praise in these years.

Dwellers of Hades and time

Picture how the dwellers of Hades envy the living for the years that they enjoy, and those which they waste. They wonder how people can disregard their salvation and not redeem their time. The rich man asked our father Abraham to send a messenger to his family in the world to warn them from what he suffers in Hades.

Picture also if one of those dwellers of Hades had the chance to return back to life for a few weeks! What would he do? How would he live? No doubt he will not waste one second without yielding fruit.

In the lives of the desert fathers, we read about one of the saintly pious elder, who, at the time of his departure, was weeping. When the monks around him asked him how much more time he needed, he answered them, "even one day." So they asked "What would you do in that day more than what you had done all your life?" He replied, "Even if I am not able to do anything, I would at least weep!!"

People's lifespan in the ancient days reached hundreds of years. Nowadays, our years are few and evil, requiring plenty of struggle. For that reason, when the devil tried to trick a saintly father to pity himself as he still had many years to live (25 years), the elder thanked him for warning him that he needed to struggle more as he had thought he had fifty years left in his life!

Furthermore, there are some moments in a man's life which mean a lot, such as the moment when one decides on monasticism or to quit a bad habit or a sin, or a moment of exceptional speech. This moment could match or surpass many years of idleness. Likewise, destinies of nations can be determined with a word which lasted for seconds.

What you could not accomplish today in hours may not be accomplished in months at a later stage of your life. Whoever toils in his young age will rejoice in his old age. Additionally, it is a sin to stop working when you are able. The one who received the one talent was not chastised because he lost it but because he did not invest it (Matthew 25). We must know that the greatest gift we have now is our own existence. We pray daily, in the thanksgiving prayer, giving thanks to God for He has brought us to this hour, for many had been amongst us last year but today they are not, others were alive a few hours ago but now they are counted amongst the dead. Time redeemed with toil and spiritual fruit when compared to eternity is likened to a drop of water when compared to an ocean or like a grain of sand when compared to the vast desert.

E - Evil days

St. Paul points to the evil days as the reason for the necessity to redeem the time. As many enemies and perditions surround us, we must watch and realize the great risk we are in, otherwise, we will easily be overtaken by this immensity of evil.

For the days are evil

I cannot tell whether days are becoming more evil with time, or whether man is maturing in wickedness! Did people turn wicked because of the evil world? Or did the world become evil because of man's wickedness? This wickedness started very early in human history. The Lord said to Adam after his fall, "Cursed is the ground for your sake" (Genesis 3:17). In the book of Genesis, we read, "Then the Lord saw that the wickedness of man was great in the earth, and that every intent of the thoughts of his heart was only evil continually. And the Lord was sorry that He had made man on the earth, and He was grieved in His heart" (Genesis 6:5-6).

In the dawn of the New Testament, St. Paul instructs, "Let us lay aside every weight, and the sin which so easily ensnares us" (Hebrews 12:1). Since the beginning of humanity, sin offered itself to man in many forms; lust of all sorts, corruption, seeking indulgence by all means, violence, enmity, and seventeen more forms of sin mentioned by St Paul. He says, "Now the works of the flesh are evident, which are;

adultery, fornication, uncleanness, lewdness, idolatry, sorcery, hatred, contentions, jealousies, outbursts of wrath, selfish ambitions, dissensions, heresies, envy, murder, drunkenness, revelries, and the like of which I tell you beforehand, just as I told you in time past, that those who practice such things will not inherit the kingdom of God" (Galatians 5:19-21).

Moreover, the days are evil for the surprises that daily enter our hearing, sight, and emotions. We hear and read of many shocking unexpected news and horrible accidents, which would have never crossed our minds. We hear of strange crimes these days like parents killing their own children, children their parents, students their teachers, and teachers their students. We also hear of the horrifying outspread of immorality and drugs, and the appalling websites that generate from unknown sources. It has come to a point that the everyday realities of wickedness and crime has become more terrifying than those in horror movies and books. Unfortunately, crime has become the norm of our news' front stories, and people are not even attentive to them anymore due to their frequency.

What makes days evil as well are the conceptions that get obscure with time, such as sin becoming habit and being treated as normal behavior. As St. John writes, the world lies in wickedness; "We know that we are of God and the whole world lies under the sway of the wicked one" (1 John 5:19).

This is because the devil is the prince of this world, and he is evil, a liar and the source of all evil. He complains against the children of God and sows in them contentions. He incites wicked people against the righteous, and meanwhile, he startles and doubts the righteous. "He speaks from his own resources for he is a liar and the father of it" (John 8:44).

Our life on earth is imperfect and unstable. Whoever wants to secure his future has to abide by righteousness and adhere to Christ and not to this evil and imperfect world. As St. Paul instructs, "Set your mind on things above, not on things on the earth" (Colossians 3:2).

Salt of the earth. Light of the world

However, it is possible for man to live in uprightness even in the midst of this wicked world. It is like a ship which travels through the sea, floating in it, without having water enter it and sink it. For example, David was a blessing to his generation, "For David after he had served his own generation by the will of God, fell asleep, was buried with his fathers" (Acts 13:36). On the other hand, there is another who may get taken by the current, so his days become evil, but he adds evil to his life and he himself becomes wicked. We then have two kinds of people:

- One who suffers for he is righteous and the days are evil

- One who makes the righteous suffer for he is wicked

It is strange that people suffer and groan because of the evil days, but they do not question why it is evil. Do they have anything to do with this evil? One person can turn his evil surroundings into an environment of peace, love and joy, while another can do the exact opposite.

We read about Lot the righteous and how he was tormented by the wickedness that surrounded him. "For that righteous man, dwelling among them, tormented his righteous soul from day to a day by seeing and hearing their lawless deeds" (2 Peter 2:8). Lot, however, remained upright, striving fervently and thus he was crowned by God.

Lastly: The good days

We can make the days good for those who live with us by lifting their burdens through our good deeds. It is as a stranger in a city whose sojourning in it is a blessing, joy, and comfort to those whom he lives amongst. They do not forget him and his name becomes bound with goodness. A righteous and virtuous man can turn a whole city to God. The Lord declared before the exile to Babel that He was ready to forgive Jerusalem if one righteous person was found in it (Jeremiah 5:1-2). Furthermore, an upright person can turn his room, and even his home into the holiest place on earth.

7

Self-Examine

Introduction

Self-examination is a necessity for the spiritual growth. In fact, the lack of it is the reason for consistent and repetitive falling and the lack of sensitivity towards sin. Inability and neglect of self-examination makes us unable to turn our life events into spiritual experiences that could further our spiritual life. To some extent, it could meet God's judgement towards us as well as the judgment of others. As St. Isaac said, "reconcile with yourself, and heaven and earth will reconcile with you."

Self-examination shifts our interest from judging others. Whoever falls in judging others is in fact unmindful of himself as he misses the chance to uncover his sins and to realize to what level he has lapsed.

Whoever thrives in examining himself is able to have compassion on others. Moreover, every rushed poor choice was not preceded by self-examination.

By examining ourselves, we enter into our depths, to that place in which others cannot examine. St. Macarius said, "My brother, judge yourself before you be judged, for God alone is the Judge"

Self-examination is essential to the sacrament of repentance and confession, in which the Holy Spirit is present.

We remember St. Taees, St. Paiesa, and many others who reached the kingdom of heaven with a profound self-examination that led them to a sincere repentance. Thus self-examination is both a review of the goal and a correction of the path.

LORD, teach me to examine myself just as I judge others, and to love all as I love myself.

Self-examination is a pause of time

"Now my days are swifter than a runner" (Job 9:25).

Whoever discovers that time flies by and is quick to end knows that self-examining puts a pause to time, that time to which we are willingly tied, which stealthily takes us from a year to another. Time snatches from us what is ours: the youth and its strong will, the days of power and simplicity, the days of offering and giving. How difficult it is to awaken in our old age when we are in need of someone to take us to church, or to read us the Bible, or to speak to us about repentance. Indeed, it will be as it's said, "their words seemed to them like idle tales, and they didn't believe them" (Luke 24:11).

When we pause time, it is just as a camera which captures a picture of a high speed train or a flying aircraft. Despite the high speed of the train, the camera could stop it and capture it in fine details, and as a result, we can spot the specifics. In that same manner, you shall examine yourself saying with St. Arsenious, "what did we do of what pleases God and what did we do of what does not please God?" and with St.

Nestarion, "what did we do according to God's will and what was against His will?"

Ask yourself what in direction are you going? To where is this path taking you? Is that what God wills? Will you be saved if you continue this way? Were you pleasant with whom you had met today? Were you right or wrong in all what you spoke of? Did you cause those who heard you to stumble? Did your day pass properly or haphazardly or as you wanted for it to go? Was your day for Christ? Or did Satan seize it? How many times did you fall? How many times did you indulge in unholy thoughts? How many people were stumbled by you? And how many benefited from you regarding their salvation? What is the conclusion of the day? Do you feel regret or satisfaction?

What if time goes back?

What if the past twenty-four hours did not happen and the events of that day were just a dream? A very long dream?[110] Would you take the same actions? Answer the same way? What about your zeal in the spirit? Would you pray for a perfect spiritual day? Your speech, your comments? Would you control yourself and your mind? Would you flee from whatever would drag you to acts of foolishness?

Give thanks, then, to the Lord, the Longsuffering.

God's longsuffering

"And consider that the longsuffering of our Lord is salvation" (2 Peter 3:15).

---

[110] Scientists say that a long dream takes only 3 seconds

The Lord is very patient with you; he granted you a new day. As if He gives you a whole twenty-four hours, as a daily allowance, to achieve whatever you could not the day before. In one of those hours, you can accomplish what others cannot do or even what you previously could not have done in months.

A true fighter can accomplish in few hours that which was done by those who started years before him. Likewise, one can lose years of struggle and labor in one hour.

A saint once said, "a person can gain in one hour what another cannot gain in years, that is if the first is zealous while the second is slothful in his intent."

Be confident that God would never give up on you! You may give up on yourself, others may give up on you, or perhaps you on them. You may even lose hope of God's mercy. But no doubt, God still loves you and still trusts you.

Make today better than yesterday and tomorrow better than today

"Forgetting those things which are behind and reaching forward to those things which are ahead" (Philippians 3:13).

When you retreat to yourself when the day is over, know that you are required to get ready for a new day. The day has already passed with its good and its bad. Now, turn all of its events into spiritual insight that can be of assistance to you tomorrow. What you fell into today, either by ignorance, forgetfulness, or weakness, you will pay attention to it tomorrow. As one of the fathers once said, "I don't recall that the devil ensnared me twice in the same matter."

Once, the great philosopher Socrates was accused with a grim accusation. He then said to his disciple, "They wrongfully condemned us, thus let us carry on with our lives in a way that proves them wrong."

We ought to know that we might be also judged on what we did not do, not only what we did. This gives self-examination a positive dimension, making it open to a lot more than just rebuke and despair.

Resolve, tonight, that tomorrow will be of a good start. Make it count as one of the blessed days in your life that imprints you with godly remembrances, like peace yielded by prayer, or endurance accepting the slap on your face with gladness, or exercising kindness or fortifying your mind and heart against the devil.

A fitting day for repentance

"That now is a high time to awake out of sleep" (Romans 13:11).

When you retreat to yourself, consider that today is the most suitable day to repent and to start a new life. Do not regard the thoughts that tell you that tomorrow will a better chance to repent, as this is a diabolic scheme of stalling; presenting no repentance the day before proves to you this warfare.

Therefore, when you feel the need to examine yourself, do not delay, because only a few seconds could stand between intensity and loss of yearning. You lose yearning if you delay turning it into a spiritual gain. Moreover, if you try to find it later, you will not be able to. Only then, self-examination will turn into a routine that is void of any outcome.

One of the desert fathers was confronted by the devil who, in false compassion, said to him, "Have mercy on yourself! Why are you exercising harsh asceticism and long vigils? You still have twenty-five more years in this life." The father answered saying, "Then I have to double my work, as I thought I had another fifty years." St. Isaac said, "Everyday, consider that you only have this day in life, thus you won't sin in it."

Hope

"No sin can overcome God's love to mankind"- Abba Peter

Do not boast. Satan may actually push you to examine yourself, even to condemn yourself, until you reach despair and low self-esteem. He does this sometimes if he failed previously in driving you to vainglory. Therefore, it is necessary that self-examination and hope walk hand in hand. We should not disregard God's role in our repentance and our progress in the spiritual path. We unite our will with God's will for our salvation and we offer the desire and He, in turn, grants us the ability. We offer the intent and He grants the expense. Our own existence until this day is an icon of hope, for every morning is a message of hope from God telling us that He still believes in our honest desire to repent and to live with Him.

It is essential, when you examine yourself, to absorb that divine fusion of blame and hope. Condemnation, void of hope, is clear satanic work. Be on guard! The same devil who lectures you about God's mercy, love and hope when you are faced by sin, is the same devil that declares perdition and dreadfulness of sin when you befall in it. It is not the end of the world if we sin but we are to humbly resolve to quit sinning. The Lord will not condemn us because we sinned, but he will if we did not repent after we have sinned. This is how self-examination puts an end to a chain of falls.

"I will plead my case against you, because you say I have not sinned" (Jeremiah 2:35)

New Year's Eve

Every time you examine yourself, consider it as New Year's Eve—an end for a year and the start of another. During your visits to the monasteries,[111] you may have noticed that the monks do not celebrate New Year's Eve, considering that every night is the start for a new year—a new year of The Lord, which starts with self-examination. St. Gregory the theologian mentions that the Christians in his days used to examine themselves on the eve of Epiphany every year to renew their blessed vows that they had offered to the Lord on the eve of their baptism.

Repentance is not seasonal and this is why monasteries do not hold spiritual revivals and sermons during fasting days as churches do. Even on the feasts of the monastery's patron saint, monastics celebrate only the day of the feast with a vigil of prayers and praises. This is because a monk's daily exercise is to always examine himself, without having a specific season for it. Unlike those who live in the world, who feel the urge for self-examination at the end of their day for instance, a monk merely and unceasingly watches himself. We read in The Paradise of the Fathers about a saint who turned self-examination into a daily task, and he tied his only daily meal to its outcome, which on some days made him deny eating.[112]

St Isaac said, "Do not count it a day of your life the day which passes without you retreating to yourself, reflecting on your mistakes and falls

---

[111] Till recent times New Year's Eve was a night like any other, but now because of the many visitors in these seasons, monasteries started organizing spiritual vigils.
[112] Abba Siluan – Paradise of the fathers

and rectifying yourself. Woe to him who does not weep, regret, or purge his blemishes as long as there is time for repentance."

Moreover, you should not seek to know when the end of days is, regarding each day as the last day in your life. Man usually dies in a day unknown to him, and he may even be taken forcibly. The saints who knew the day of their departure did not actually need to know it, as St. Anthony said, "Consider every day as the last one for you on earth, and that will save you from sinning." St. Isaac also said, "Each day should be regarded as the only one left for you in the world, this way you avoid sinning."

To each of us, the end of the world is the end of our life and this should be always on our mind. We read about Amma Sarah when she said, "I put one foot on a step to go up and I imagine that death will come faster than me moving the other foot."

However, it may be suitable for a beginner to determine specific times to examine himself.

What would happen if God sent an angel to a person telling him that he will depart in few hours? What would he do in these few hours? What more than weeping? It may be due to his tremendous joy if he is ready, or it may be as the most fitting expression of his repentance from his sins if he is fearful.

He would not delay in repenting, "redeeming the time", because repentance is two-sided. One side, weeping and regretting, is internal, while the other, which is struggling and enduring, is external. St. John Climacus said, "No one can pick a day to live perfectly unless he considers it as the last day in his life."

Honesty with oneself

The human soul is mysterious, and one needs openness and honesty to realize its being. We usually present ourselves to others in a perfect image which abides by decency, courtesy and politeness, while we could be the complete opposite in the comfort of our own privacy. Our own room is the safe place where, within its walls, we act in liberty as no one is watching and there is no fear of making others stumble. There, we may let ourselves do whatever we would never dare to do in the presence of others, whether in church or in our community in general.

We should acknowledge that in our own privacy, we return to our normal dimension without cover-up or hypocrisy, because a lot of our acts and expressions are ruled by society, norms, and personal pride. Sometimes, we fear people more than the Lord!

In actuality, we should accomplish both matters. The first is that our attitude towards others be proper and according to God's commandment and the lives of the saints, and the second, is that to transfer that attitude to our own room and between our close ones.

Let us endeavor to make honesty and truthfulness the base when we examine ourselves. A sin could go unnoticed by others, because of God's love and covering, as well as your skills! Beware of forgiving yourself for it, but rather, judge yourself for what has gone unnoticed by others. Moreover, do not blame others for being the reason for your fall.

When you condemn yourself, do not have self-pity. Offer yourself a sacrifice to Christ, when you retreat to self-examination. St. Pachomius said, "Set yourself aside, as a wise ruler, to judge your thoughts, keeping what you find beneficial and proper while casting away what is harmful."

In your room, you will realize your true self. You may deceive others to gain their respect and flattery, but do not deceive yourself. One can have people's approval and praise while God sees them in an entirely different way and vice versa.

Try to write down all your sins, whether action, thought, or speech. Hold yourself accountable for what you wrote, telling yourself meekly, "This is me, even if people did not realize it." As it is mentioned in the Bible, "Our sins testify against us" (Isaiah 59:12).

Nevertheless, you can write the good which God fulfilled through you. Do this to give thanks to The Lord, as well as to avoid falling in low self-esteem.

But what is the standard to which we self-examine?

Our Lord Jesus Christ

"Leaving us an example that you should follow Him" (1 Peter 2:21).

We take our Lord Jesus Christ as a reference and as a standard when we examine ourselves. We measure our actions to His standard. We should ask ourselves, would the Lord Christ—Glory be to Him—have behaved as I behaved today? Would He have had the same reaction? Would He have had the same position as I had?

The Lord Christ was a "Perfect Man", as we say in the midnight praises, "*Hos romi enti leos,*" meaning he was wise, sincere, kind, hospitable, friendly, social, and all that entails complete perfection.

"Till we all come to the unity of the faith and of the knowledge of the Son of God, to a perfect man, to the measure of the stature of the fullness of Christ" (Ephesians 4:13).

We bow down to God regretting our deeds, as we find out that we had tainted His Image, and we have not been witnesses and ambassadors to Him this past day. Remember to ask God fervently to help you in the coming day to make others see Him in you.

Examine yourself in the light of the life of our Lord Jesus Christ and according to the lives of the saints who strived to be in His likeness. Purify your heart to make it more fitting for the dwelling of God. Along the day, try to see God instead of your wisdom in every word and every action.

"He who says he abides in Him ought himself also to walk just as He walked" (1 John 2:6)

Notes about the past day

"Give an account of your stewardship" (Luke 16:2)

After your self-examination, write down your remarks: what you have done and what God has done to you throughout the day. Afterwards, write down a prayer of thanks, expressing joy that the Lord has granted you a new start.

Also, you can summarize your notes to use as pointers in your confession, so that you do not forget your sins and to be worthy of partaking of Holy Communion. One other benefit of these notes is to discern whether you are growing or whether you are lapsing.

Self-examination seasons

As previously mentioned, while self-examination has times and seasons to those who live in the world, it is rather the main concern for those who live in the wilderness and to those who dedicate themselves to purify their heart and senses.

Seasons for self-examination:

1. Daily session at the end of each day. Keep a journal with your daily notes, to monitor your progress.

2. While getting ready for confession (At least once a month), revisit your journal to remind yourself.

3. Write down monthly notes which will help you review the whole year at the end.

4. On New Year's Eve, give an account for the whole year. Take up a resolution, for instance, to make the new year a year of humility, or a of obedience or of almsgiving or of asceticism, etc. focusing all your readings, prayers, and exercises on this virtue. Keep in mind that every year's virtue will be an addition to the previous, and not a substitute. That is how the saints lived.

Self-examination and confession

These steps should be taken before confession:

1. Examine yourself to discover your sins, negligence, and short comings.

2. Condemn yourself for the sin, but always accompany this with hope in Christ.

3. Repent. The difference between self-condemnation and repentance is that the first is regretting our deeds while the second is truthfully vowing to strive not to repeat them.

4. Confess before God, asking for forgiveness of the past and support for the future

5.   Finally, confess before the church (the priest), which is considered a declared repentance or the pronounced component of repentance.

Self-examination as an everyday life virtue

In light of living according to the commandment, self-examination becomes a dock in all life aspects. For example, a watchful and honest merchant will stop every now and then to check if his trade is going accordingly with his plan, if there any weak points or illegality, if he owes any taxation or if he is due anything. Any buyer can be easily cheated, but the seller should not deceive or take advantage of anyone! One should not consider that judging himself on what others or God judged him is enough. Man does not need chastisement or incarceration to repent, consequently, our conscience should not move according to what people say but according to the Holy Spirit and the Bible.

Some may take advantage of the fact that their sins and transgressions went unnoticed, so they merely pass by them as if they did not happen. God in other times permits that they become punished for sins they have not committed. In turn, whoever feels that he is being punished for what he has not done should remember instantly the sins which went unpunished whether by people or by himself. Even if he dodged punishment of himself or of others, he will not flee Judgment Day, when he will be ashamed before all. Therefore, we hear of the repentant saint who was asked to bring everything she owned from her sinful life and to burn them all in front of everyone as a sign of her sincere repentance. She obeyed saying, "If all of this occurred to me here, how much greater will it be in the end (if she hadn't repented)?"

What applies to a merchant applies as well a student. He should ask himself if he was faithful in his studies or not, how much he has advanced and how much more to go, whether he used his time wisely, how honest he was in his exams, etc. And when he passes, was he worthy of it, did he really benefit from his studies in his everyday life, or did he study only to gather material for his exams and forget about them later.

So whoever conducts himself in dishonesty is actually misleading himself. This is why self-examination becomes essential to one's peace and beneficial for the future here on earth and in eternity.

Likewise, a lawyer who lies to defend and to prove the innocence of his client while he knows of his lies and of his client's punishable deeds. A lawyer's job is to defend the truth and not just to win the case. A saint once said, "Who tries to take over others using his speech, shows that the fear of God is not in him."

What applies to a lawyer applies as well to a judge.

The offender himself should not depend on what the prosecutor or the attorney says, but he should earnestly examine himself to determine the nature of his deeds. If he was to blame, he should say with the right thief, "We receive the due reward of our deeds," and should endure his punishment with gratitude. If he was not to blame, he should consider it a blessing and a cleansing sent to him from God, or a saving from what could have been worse. No doubt God will defend him. Even those who lived and died in injustice, the Lord keeps their reward and they will be crowned in front of all.

St. Augustine compares between the three young men who were saved from fire and the Maccabees who were martyred by fire saying, "God saved the young men visibly while he crowned the Maccabees invisibly." That is to say that God kept their reward until judgment day whereas He saved the young men to make their prosecutors believe in the living God.

Final sign for fruitful self-examination

"We know that we have passed from death to life because we love the brethren" (1 John 3:14)

Do not neglect examining yourself, and do not let a long time pass without it. Make it a daily routine starting and ending with prayer. If you let long periods of time pass without self-examination, you will focus only on the major sins and leave the others—the little foxes that spoil the vine. Always be meek and submissive to God's chastisement, regarding it as a blessing and healing, and that you deserve His discipline. Blame only yourself.

"And we indeed justly, for we receive the due reward of our deeds" (Luke 23:41).

In this manner you become cleansed and purified by self-examination.

A final sign of fruitful self-examination is not only feeling internal happiness but also feeling that you are the only sinner while all the others are righteous. It is when you feel that blessed feeling of loving everyone, purging all envy and hatred from your heart and the feeling of indescribable love stirring within you.

8

The Virtue of Asceticism

The virtue of asceticism has perhaps been associated with monks and the monastic life in the mind of many. It has likewise been associated with food and drink and deprivation. The term "ascetic", however, means discipline, and not deprivation. As a result, the ascetic person is the person who is able to discipline himself, and control his passions, and his desires.

Furthermore, what is said of a "regime" is also said of "asceticism"; for the meaning of regime to the general public is "weight loss" but it actually means a system that is followed, not necessarily pertaining to food. As such, a regimen is a system for discipline in general.[113]

---

[113] The word "ascetic" means "self-denial" or "self-discipline." The verb "exercise" means *asko* or *askeo*, that is, "train" or "strive." This word appears once in the New testament: "*This being so, I myself always strive* (askeo) *to have a conscience without offense toward God and men*" (Acts 24:16). In Coptic, it is "*ti na er <u>askin.</u>*" As to the root of the word *askeo*, it is *asitos*, wherein the alpha means "without" and *sitos* means "food," that is, fasting. The second word that is used in the Bible and that carries the same meaning, is exercise (γυμναζω), *exercise yourself toward godliness* (1 Timothy 4:7 NKJV). [The word in Arabic which is translated "exercise" in NKJV, can be translated

The word "Scetis," which refers to the most important and greatest monastic region in the world and in history, is related to asceticism. This region used to be called *Pi ma in ni askitis*, that is, "the place of the ascetics." Interestingly, this region was also called *Shiheet*, which means "the balance of the hearts," that is, the place wherein hearts are weighed. According to Palladius,[114] it is said that some monks from Scetis went to visit Amma Sarah, so she offered them food. They set the good aside and ate from what is inferior, the bad. She, then, said to them, "You are truly from Scetis." The word bears two meanings: "Ascetics" or those who belong to the place of the Ascetics (Scetis).

The difference between the poor and the ascetic is that the poor wishes and desires but he is unable to fulfill his wishes, while the ascetic may be able to but he refrains and disciplines himself. It is the difference between discipline and repression; for repression is the intensity of longing with the intensity of deprivation, while discipline is the existence of the desire with the availability of the means to fulfill it. There is, however, an enlightened will controlling the relationship between the two.

The following story reveals to us the Fathers' enlightened mind pertaining to asceticism. It happened once that Abba Sylvanus and his disciple Zachariah were visiting one of the monasteries. There, the monks set before them food, so they ate. On their way back, his disciple found water on the way, so when he wanted to drink, the saint

into "tame"]. From this, the word "gymnasium" came. In Coptic, it is (arigumnazin), that is, "he tamed."

[114] Palladius was a monk from Constantinople, who came to Egypt and lived in it for about five years in various monasteries, and he recorded what he saw and wrote the lives and sayings of a large number of fathers. He, then, sent his memoir to a friend of his named Lausus. This history and important heritage became to be widely known as "the Lausiac History" and it is known now as the Paradise of the Monks [or Fathers].

prevented him because the appointed time of their eating has not yet come! When the disciple marveled because they had actually eaten a short while before, he answered him, saying, "For the sake of love we ate, and now we should not annul our rule."

In truth, fasting was not in itself a goal in the lives of the fathers, but one of the instruments helping them on the way to God. This is, of course, regarding personal fasts and not the fixed fasts in the liturgical year to which all abide, whether in the world or the monasteries. While, as punishment, one person was subjected to keeping a personal fast by the command of the fathers, another was punished by being prevented from fasting! The goal in both cases is the same, that is, the treatment of vainglory or pride; as one who became prideful because of his asceticism, while thoughts of uncleanness weighed down on another, so he was in need of subjecting his body and mind.

The fathers say that "fasting makes the body humble." Amma Sarah says, "We prefer obedience to asceticism, for the latter brings pride but the former brings humility." A person may do everything, even what may be heavy on him, as long as it is his own wish, except obedience! Only in obedience does one cut off his desires and is carried upon the will of another. We read of St. Athanasius the Athonite, the founder of monasticism in Mount Athos, Greece, that the first order he received when he stepped up to monasticism, was to slaughter a lamb and eat it. He obeyed instantly!

Within the framework of moderation in the spiritual conduct, the fathers say that "the middle way has saved many," especially when we are beginners. Thus, we give the body its needs, but its needs only and no more! We may exceed this limit slightly, on the days we are not fasting, but this is also with measure. It is possible to put two signposts for this: the first representing *"the minimum"* which we should not go below in fasting, obeying the divine voice: "For no one ever hated his own flesh, but nourishes and cherishes it, just as the Lord does the church" (Ephesians 5:29) ; and *"the maximum"* which we should not go beyond on non-fasting days, adhering also to the verse, "But I discipline my body and bring it into subjection" (I Corinthians 9:27) .Little by little, with exercise and with guidance, the need of the body for food diminishes.

Perhaps this is suitable for the majority of monks and nuns or the consecrated. Some of them might adhere to severe asceticism—with their spiritual guide's coordination, of course, and others are lenient with themselves. Their guides might see that they ought to lighten up on themselves for a time, within the framework of the general spiritual conduct specific for them.

In the life of St. Pachomius, we read that when he had to spend a long time travelling, he asked the monk responsible for the kitchen to take care of the fathers until he returned. When he returned, he asked the monk about what he had done in his absence. The monk said to him that he had decided to help the monks in the life of asceticism and did this through shutting the kitchen so that they may eat dry bread. Meanwhile he had utilized his time in making baskets, to set aside their price for the monastery. St. Pachomius asked him to bring all the baskets he had made and put them in a pile in the monastery's yard. The pile was huge. The saint, then, ordered that the monastery's bell to be rung, so all the monastery's monks immediately came. St. Pachomius looked at the baskets then to the monk, and he said to him, "Why did you annul the natural fruit of asceticism?" He, then, ordered that all the baskets be burned before the monks.[115]

Allow me to speak frankly saying that monasticism was the strongest when it was based on solitude and not communal living. With a quick overview of history, we discover that the weakness of monasticism is tightly linked to the love of possessions. When a monk lived in his cave, alone, he acquired a personal spiritual experience with God; God would care for him, prepare for him his table, lift away from him dangers, and pour consolation into his heart. I remember when one of these solitaries was chosen for the bishopric, and after some time had passed, he noticed that he did not have the same old consolation. When he cried asking God about the reason, he was told, "When you were in your cave in the desert, you had no one but Me. I used to take care of you. Now, you have many caring for you." St Isaac, therefore, says, "Human consolations prevent divine consolations."

The monk places all his trust in God, and puts his hope upon Him. God, in return, takes care of him and becomes responsible for him; "because he has set his love upon Me, therefore I will deliver him; I will set him on high, because he has known My name." (Psalm 91:14).

Monasteries now, however, have walls and the cells are securely sealed by modern locks! There are guards and sometimes policemen. I remember the cells of old. There were no locks for them, since if a thief went in, he would find nothing worth stealing! This is a sign of the true

---

[115] The saint means that a monk, when food is set before him and he gives it up by his will, brings forth by this the fruit of asceticism. For there is a difference between the ascetic and the poor.

monk, he has nothing for which he might be treated unjustly, nor wronged on it!

I would like, in this vein, to say that the Church in general, and monasticism especially, is not a corporation nor an enterprise but a movement. The disciples left all and followed the Lord.[116] From here, then, monasticism is a Biblical way, wherein the monk hears the divine voice: "Go, sell... and come, follow Me" (Matthew 19:21).[117] St Isaac says, "The person who sets forth on monasticism, without changing first nor desisting from the care of the world and its desires and its pleasures, will not be able to become a monk, will not attain virtue, and will not be able to stand before the arrows of the enemy, which are the lusts of the soul."

One of the fathers recounted the following symbolic story, saying:

A monk asked persistently from God to guide him to a place wherein he may live away from people. God did guide him to an isolated place atop a hill in the mountains of Lebanon, where he made a hut from the branches of trees and lived therein. As winter came, he got cold. He looked around and caught a glimpse of some huts belonging to shepherds. He went down to them and entreated them to lend him a blanket, and they did so with joy. Several weeks later, He came back to them, complaining about mice destroying the blanket. They felt sorry for this and gave him another blanket...This matter happened time and time again, and so they suggested that he let a cat live with him, that perhaps the mice would fear it! He agreed and it indeed happened that the mice went away from him. Yet another problem came up which he

---

[116] See Luke 5:11, 28
[117] See also Mark 10:21 and Luke 14:25-33

had not paid attention to—the cat's food. He went down to them again, this time asking for some milk, so they gave him milk. Whenever the container of milk was consumed, he received more from them. They then suggested that they give him an ewe, so that he may milk it every morning to feed the cat that drove out the mice which destroyed his blanket. Once again, he forgot that the ewe itself was in need of food. He asked therefore the nomads to give him an ax and some seeds. He began reclaiming a small area of the land around him, that perhaps he may get some food for the poor ewe. What was marvelous was that the land produced fruit in great abundance, which encouraged him to reclaim a larger area. The reclamation project succeeded astonishingly, so it was transformed into a huge enterprise including a vast area of the land and whatever the enterprise needed, from buildings to imported machines.

One day, a visitor came to look over the products of his enterprise. The monk welcomed him ardently, taking him from one place to another, informing him about the kinds of cows they had, the local and the domesticated, and the tens of kinds of cheese and other dairy products. He, then, brought him back to his *luxurious office*, and when the guest sat, he examined the monk for a while and said to him: "Is it for this I brought you here?" It happened that the Lord Christ Himself was visiting him.

This story is symbolic and amusing, but it reveals how a man often deviates from his goal to expand horizontally, or to transform the principal goal to small equal goals! Thus a person begins in the Spirit, then is made perfect by the flesh.[118]

Kinds of asceticism

As we have agreed, asceticism as a virtue is not limited to food and drink only, as it means "discipline" in general. It is used as a term for possessions, for a monk's relationships with others, and for other aspects of the inner spiritual conduct. Let us take, as an example, another kind of asceticism, such as:

Asceticism in knowledge:

It is very important that we are aware of the difference between a computer and a human mind. We are capable of getting rid of the information that has gushed into the device by "formatting" it, while it is impossible to get rid of the unprofitable materials we have crammed into the mind. It is therefore necessary that we choose what we read and hear carefully. Otherwise, the memory's remaining capacity will gradually diminish, and when we are aware of our need of more spiritual knowledge, understanding and contemplation, we find that these secular experiences, crammed in the mind, become an obstacle.

Regarding memory, or the ability to retrieve, all we read goes into the mind and memory, and is blended with feelings, and mixes with our

---

[118] See Galatians 3:3

whole being, causing effect in one way or another. All are smelted in one pot, to give a personality, with traits changing with time according to what is being consumed. About this, some of the philosophers say, "Show me what you read; I will show you who you are." Or rather, "Show me what you re-read; I will show you who you are!" This is why monks and nuns are tonsured at a younger age, because their readiness in such an age for obedience, asceticism and toil, is much greater. Not only this, but that the mind may be serene and clear, except for some of what it has acquired from the family and from the small community (school and Church). These two circles do not present as much danger as that of the open community, full of contradictions, disparities, perversions, futile values, erroneous concepts, and evil experiences. We may even demand of the monk or the consecrated to test work (practical) life for a brief period, and this is not that he may gain that experience but that he may try himself in work. This natural line of life might be attractive for him.

A person, therefore, ought to choose what he reads with great care. He may find himself heading towards reading newspapers, magazines, and papers strewed on the road. He must practice asceticism in this too, and discipline himself to control what goes into his mind.

There were some who were accustomed to reading the daily newspapers, and others who had literary readings, political or others. They had difficulty abandoning them and renouncing them after joining the monasteries. I remember an advice we received at the start of our monastic life was that we were not to read theological books and exegesis books, so that the monk is not fought with the desire to teach and the love of authority. We used to receive theology practically through pure prayer and through love of others, for the Trinity is the Mystery of love. Theology is "to pray well," as the fathers say.

We read in the History of Palladius that a council was held in Scetis—perhaps to discuss the Origenian problem. In this council, Evagrius of Pontus stood and spoke, and he was an erudite scholar and philosopher. When he finished speaking, a father of the mountain stood and said to him, "We know, our father, that if you had been in your town, you would have become a bishop or a chief over many. But here, you are like a stranger." So he answered in humility saying, "It is true that I have spoken once, and God willing, there will not be a second."

Asceticism in conduct:

I remember also that we used to train ourselves in the first years of monasticism to not turn back when we heard a sound or footsteps behind us in one of the paths, or the sound of a machine or workers. We would say to ourselves, "What does this have to do with me!? They do their work, and we do our work."

Once, Father Isaac visited one of the elders, and there, he heard some sounds. He asked the elder, "Is there poultry here, father?" The elder in admonition answered, saying, "Why are you forcing me to talk, Isaac, those like you only hear such sounds!"

Beware lest you are doing this out of the desire for the praise of others. This leads us to speaking about another kind of asceticism.

Asceticism in the love of others for us:

Some may do good, not for the sake of God, but on account of others...
not for the glory of God, but that they may be satisfied with themselves.
One, for example, might pursue kindness as a way to deal with others,
not as a pure fruit of the Holy Spirit[119] but for the sake of receiving
praise, that it might be said of him that he is gentle or kind or loving.
Another may show a great measure of patience, or may adorn himself
with a shining smile always, only caring about others' opinion of him!

It is true that the Bible commands us to have regard for good things
in the sight of men,[120] that men may see our good works so they glorify
our Father in heaven.[121] It is of necessity, however, that what is manifest
on the outside be a reflection of what is in the heart, and diligence
should be taken that we do not cause others to stumble, especially the
weak and the unenlightened. If it were not so, then, while what is
manifest inspires humility, poverty, and forgiveness, the sin of pride is
lying in wait within, unconcerned since its nourishment is delivered to
it regularly!

St. Paul says, "For not he who commends himself is approved, but
whom the Lord commends." (2 Corinthians 10:18). Moreover, the
fathers say, "Behold, men die and their honors die with them." I say this
that we may be cautious of those from whom we receive honor and
vainglory. Though the problem does not lie in the praise of men for us,

---

[119] Galatians 5:22
[120] See Romans 12:17
[121] See Matthew 5:16

as they are simple and pure, the danger lies in our accepting the praise, our happiness in it, and the pursuit for more of it.

As a result, we ought to give up love of praise and honor, and practice asceticism even in this, not caring about others' opinion of us. Otherwise, our journey will come to a halt. Why do we diligently run after others' opinion of us? Is it not more fitting of us that we care about God's opinion of us? Is it not dangerous that our priority is the judgement of men? Did not the Lord Christ say to us with His pure mouth, "Woe to you when all men speak well of you" (Luke 6:26). That is, if you are able to obtain the favor of all men and their praise and if you are able to change color and satisfy all tendencies and temperaments, then you are a hypocrite. Amma Sarah says, "People have many wills, so if I desired to satisfy all people, I would find myself astray at the door of each one."

When St. Theodore, the disciple of St. Pachomius, declared that a person ought to be "round, not with horns or square,"[122] he meant that a man ought to be malleable, easy to deal with, easy to win over, a sweet company, not moved with every wind.[123]

There are two things we must abide by, in this context:

The first is that we should not hurt anyone. The second is that we should not occupy ourselves with how much others love us or how

---

[122] A similar saying is attributed to Abba Muthues: "Now, he who sits among the brethren must not possess four corners, but he must be altogether round, so that he may move smoothly in respect of every man." PHF, Vol. II, Apo. 512.
[123] See Ephesians 4:14

much they hate us, or with people's opinion in general; that is, *"Do not have your peace in people's mouths."*

On the contrary, many of the fathers endeavored to show what people would despise them. St. Poemen, for example, pretended foolishness and craziness before the ruler who had come to visit him and take his blessing. We, as beginners, however, should not walk in this conduct, lest it gives the opposite result, for it is a way teeming with dangers, not appropriate for the statures of beginners.

John Cassian wrote about St. Paphnutius, who used to live in a monastery in Pelusium (near Port Said), that when he became renowned, he wanted to escape the visitors thronging him. At first, he thought of not leaving his cell, but he feared that people might congregate around it and force him to leave it. He, then, thought of leaving the monastery for another, but he decided against the idea lest they discover his new location and follow him there. Finally, he got the idea to hide in a layman's garb going to another place. He did so and went towards Upper Egypt, walking for long until he stopped at the door of one of St. Pachomius' monasteries. When he rang the monastery's bell, the monk who was the doorkeeper came out. St. Paphnutius told him that he was a man whose sojourn in the world has been prolonged, and that he desired now to spend the rest on his life as a monk, as he was approaching sixty years of age. The monk apologized to him for his old age, but then he left him and shut the door, leaving him outside. Two days later, the monk opened the door to find Abba Paphnutius still sitting beside the door, so he marveled at that. Again, he begged him greatly to let him join the monastery, even as one of the workers. Finally, the monk agreed, so they made him work in the garden of the monastery. There, he worked in humility and obedience to a young monk.

One day, while a monk from Pelusium was visiting that place, he caught a glimpse of Abba Paphnutius in the garden of the monastery, so he knew him immediately though he had laymen clothing on. The Abba entreated him not to tell anyone in the monastery, but he hastened and notified them. Enlightened, they offered apologies and honored him. When he decided to leave the monastery, they accompanied him with timbrels and incense. He ran away afterwards to a cave wherein St. Jerome lived, near Bethlehem. Eventually, they brought him again to Pelusium, and there, he passed away after a short time.

Inward pride is nourished by outward honor, which a person accepts, and permits to go inside his mind and heart. Thus, we must reject all honor coming to us from the world, for we are most aware of our weaknesses and deficiencies. God in His compassion has covered us and has not exposed us before others. The philosopher Diogenes said, reproaching Alexander the Great, "Life, whose end is this, renouncing it is far better."

Love of possessions:

If we were to abide by the genuine teaching we have received from the fathers, non-possessiveness then is the trait of the true Christian; he is satisfied with enough food that allays the hunger and with clothing that covers his nakedness. If all his possessions were to be stolen, there would be nothing for him to feel sorrow for, as what is important is a man's soul, his inner content, and not what he stores around him like the rich fool.[124] The wise rich man is he whose concern is his love for Christ, his love for others, and his inward adorning. As for the rich fool, it is he who puts his hope and trust upon the riches of the world.

There lived in the Baramos monastery a monk called Fr. Tadros Abba Paul. He used to keep a small wooden box outside his cell, and the monks would put food for him in it, and his portion of what was distributed from the blessing to the monks. Most of the time, he would leave whatever was in the box until it was spoiled. If he wanted to eat something, he would go out and eat some of what was left for him in humility. He never brought food into his cell as he had in his cell more important work!

I remember also visiting a monk in his cell, and there I noticed that he possessed no books but only one or two which he had put on top of the mat to read. When I asked him if he kept a library in his cell, he answered that every book in his cell which he did not read was a witness and judge against him! It is also said that one of the elders once rebuked a monk because he had kept many books and manuscripts in his cell. He said to him: "You have taken the food of the poor and with it have filled the windows of your cell!"

The more a person is enlightened and becomes full from within, the more he renounces what is around him. His Holiness Pope Shenouda III recounts the following story about the love of possessions:

---

[124] Luke 12:16-21

One time, one of the monastic elders passed away, and his cell was full of many things, some necessary and others, ordinary and unimportant. As soon as the father was buried in the cemetery of the monastery, the Abbot of the monastery said to the fathers, "Whoever has need of anything from this cell, let him take it." In a few minutes, most of the fathers were returning to their cells with something in their hands from the cell, for a blessing. A few hours had not passed his departure before his cell became completely vacant of its content, even so that some monks undertook to cleaning it and preparing it for another monk to live in!

I would like to say that God treats us two ways concerning need: either *providing* for the need or *dropping* the need.

In the first, God fulfills what we need of food, drink, and other matters. In this regard, throughout the history of monasticism, monks have innumerable experiences which they recount with joy. How could God abandon a people who have left the world for His sake, not granting sustenance for them? In the second way, He makes the monk transcend to the point where he is not occupied with food, drink or any of the affairs of this present world. The fathers' experience in fasting was to be occupied with what is more important, and time would pass in prayer, contemplation, work, and praise, before the monk would discover at the end of the day, even two, that he had not eaten. He, then, would eat a small portion of food to allay his hunger only. This is the case regarding possessions.

Fr. Abdel Messih the Ethiopian lived in a cave near Baramos monastery for thirty-eight years, without having a door or window. When Fr Antonious El Souriany (His Holiness Pope Shenouda) offered to make a door for it, Fr. Abdel Messih did not approve, saying, "does the wolf make a door for his cave? I am like the wolf, so don't be concerned about me from the wolves!"

Likewise lived St. Mary of Egypt in the wilderness, naked; and so did St. Abba Nopher the Anchorite, and the monks whom St. Macarius met at the lake.

We read in the history of Palladius that a monk came to the Church of the Cells, wearing a head cover that came down to his shoulders. When Abba Isaac, the Presbyter of the Cells, saw him, he followed him, saying, "Here monks live, but you are a man of the world, so you have no place to live here."

The cramming of our closets, our drawers, and our pantries with what exceeds the need, is against faith—faith that God is the One sustaining us. "Is not life more than food? ... Is not the body more than clothing?" (Matthew 6:25). For the One who has granted life is capable of granting sustenance, which is far easier, and so He does with the clothing for the body. St. Paul says, "As poor, yet making many rich; as having nothing, and yet possessing all things." (2 Corinthians 6:10)

In a book about prayer, a story was recounted of an elderly monk in Mount Athos. A priest who was visiting the monastery passed by him, and he found him pecking into a hard rock with a small hammer and an iron pick. When he asked him about what he was doing, he answered him that he intended on carving a hole in which to collect water when it rained, because he thirsted the year before!

The following lines will, perhaps, clarify and summarize the essence of the monastic life, as the forefathers lived it and passed it down to their disciples. It was recounted in the Paradise of the Fathers of St. Bessarion, "that he was as the birds of the heaven, as one of the beasts of the wilderness, and as the creeping things of the earth. He completed his life in tranquility, with no concern; he never cared for a home, did not store up food, nor possessed a garment or a book; but was in everything free of the passions of the body, riding atop the power of faith, becoming in the hope like a captive of the things to come; wandering in the deserts as one who has lost his way, naked under the air of heaven. And he would endure tribulations with joy."

Finally:

Hold fast to Christ, for in Him is sufficiency, and He is able to satisfy your hearts, to make you not need anything that is in this world. Inner hunger is not satisfied except by Christ, the Owner of the treasures of wisdom. For in Him is the rest we seek, the peace we sing, the joy we miss, and the tranquility we desire. As for the goods of this passing world, they are unable to accomplish for us what we would like to attain. In the Wednesday Psali of the midnight praises we say:

> "If we are needy for the money of this world,
> And we have nothing to offer as alms.
> Yet we truly have the precious pearl of great price,
> Which is the sweet name full of glory, of our Lord Jesus Christ.
> We do not ask for the wealth of this world,
> But for the salvation of our souls,
> By calling upon His holy name."

9

The Virtue of Thanksgiving

Thanksgiving is the approach of the Church in her relation with God. With it we begin all our prayers whether liturgical (as group worship) or individual prayers. As we do in; the raising of incense, the liturgy, all the sacraments of the church, each hour of the Agpeya, all ordinations, any opening of festivals or projects, and the blessing of houses. The Thanksgiving prayer fits even to be prayed during quick visits, or when we are in a hurry or a rush. Our own personal prayers start with giving thanks, and it is the first prayer we teach our children.

Thanksgiving sets the stage for the rest of our conversation with God, where we will offer our petitions, ask for forgiveness, complain to Him, or praise Him, "Continue earnestly in prayer, being vigilant in it with thanksgiving" (Col 2:4). Whether He answers us our prayers or not, we thank Him beforehand because we know that He loves us and does what is best for us, and as we thank Him in advance, we place our needs at His feet.

The meaning of the word "Thanksgiving:"

In Coptic, the thanksgiving prayer starts with the phrase: "Ⲙⲁⲣⲉⲛϣⲉⲡϩⲙⲟⲧ ⲛⲧⲟⲧϥ ⲉⲙⲉϥⲛⲟⲧⲏ" [transliterated: *Marensepehmot entotf emefnotee*], which means, "we accept grace of the hand of God." Thanksgiving is accepting what comes from the Hand of God to us regardless of the nature of the gift and whether it is according to our will or not.

There are always two ways we can fathom the gifts of God; one way is human and the other is divine. Although God always grants us what is good for us, yet we sometimes only see the opposite, and as a result, we murmur and complain. This contradiction between our will and the will of God causes us to despair and doubt God's love. God does not always explain His will and providence, especially when we murmur and complain. This is why our Lord Jesus Christ said to our teacher Peter when he rejected that He washes his feet, "What I am doing you do not understand now, but you will know after this" (John 13:7).

Accepting the gifts of God thankfully increases these gifts, as the fathers said, "There is no gift without increase, except that without thanksgiving," and, "The thanksgiving of him who takes moves the giver to give more."

Let Us Give Thanks to the Beneficent:

Sometime in the 1960s, there was a man who worked in a factory, and one day he lost one of his knuckles. This accident had a great impact on him; he was upset with God and saw the matter as a lack of love and care from God. He always questioned, "Why me? Why not someone else? Why did it have to happen altogether?" He stayed home for months before he was able to resume his work, and he was always trying to hide the hand with the missing knuckle.

One day, as he was passing through a deserted place, where some sorcerers gathered thinking they had found a treasure, which could not be opened without a human sacrifice. He was attacked by them, they siezed him and started to prepare him to be slaughtered. As they examined him, they noticed his missing knuckle and suddenly they stopped. They could no longer offer him as a sacrifice since the sacrifice had to be whole. This same missing knuckle, for which he had murmured against God, saved him, and the sad accident of losing his knuckle had become the reason his life was spared.

God only knows and only does what is good. He is the Magnificent Wonderworker, "You show loving-kindness to thousands" (Jeremiah 32:18). Throughout the Holy Bible, we see many times the phrase: *God is Good*. We praise and thank Him daily for He is Good, "O give thanks to the Lord: for He is good and virtuous, Alleluia, His mercy endures forever" (Ps 106:1). We should know that the word "Aghathon" which means "Good" in Greek, also means "Virtuous," which affirms that the Good is Virtuous and goodness is virtue. "I will freely sacrifice to You; I will praise Your name, O Lord, for it is good" (Psalm 54:6).

The Merciful God:

The heart of God is filled with mercy towards the entire creation, not just to humans, but his mercy extends to all creatures: beasts, birds, reptiles, and fish. He grants all their food in due season. He adorns the creation with inexplicable beauty and beaming colors. A close look at the skin of a snake, the complex colors of a butterfly, or the colorful pattern of the fish incites astonishment, and leads us to thank God the

Glorious. Even the grass of the field, Christ refers to it saying, "Now if God so clothes the grass of the field, which today is, and tomorrow is thrown into the oven, will He not much more clothe you, O you of little faith?" (Matthew 6:30). God adorns it with unfathomable beauty, "Consider the lilies, how they grow: they neither toil nor spin; and yet I say to you, even Solomon in all his glory was not arrayed like one of these" (Luke 12:27).

Here, I wonder how people love some of these creatures and not others; they pet some and hunt others; they kill some and disregard others, whereas God loves all and cares for all.

While God is merciful to us, tolerant to our weaknesses, and forgiving to our sins when we repent, we on the other hand, are cruel and do not have mercy towards one another. If we were to take the place of God, we would have likely burned entire cities to the ground daily. In the parable of the unforgiving servant, we find that while the master had entirely forgiven his servant who owed ten thousand talents just because he asked for compassion and patience, this same servant did not have mercy on his brother who owed him only a hundred denarii (the ratio is 1:60). He threw his brother in prison. When the master heard this, he called that cruel servant and rebuked him saying, "You wicked servant! I forgave you all that debt because you begged me. Should you not also have had compassion on your fellow servant, just as I had pity on you?" (Matthew 18:32-33).

Therefore, if we have mercy on others, we shall obtain the mercy of God. God's mercy and His longsuffering is what inspires us to have compassion on others. We let go of the very little we hold against our brothers for the many we owe God. Truly says our Lord, "Therefore be merciful, just as your Father also is merciful" (Luke 6:36).

May our hearts move with mercy towards the entire creation to have pity on all, to have tender mercies, and to have a kind heart that cannot bear seeing cruelty, weakness or pain.

There are those whose merciful hearts have moved them towards the sick... Others have established associations to take care of animals. Others have supported the environment, establishing natural reserves. "Blessed are the merciful, for they shall obtain mercy" (Matthew 5:7).

But Why Do We Give Thanks?

In true thanksgiving, we thank God for everything, concerning everything and in everything, which means:

- For everything we have gone through
- Concerning everything we live through
- And for everything we will go through.

Giving thanks to God is constant and has become our praise all day long and every day, but why do we give thanks?[125]

The Thanksgiving Prayer, which we repeat three times during the divine liturgy (vespers, matins, and during the offering), seven times during the Agpeya prayers, and during all occasions as mentioned before, is to remind us that our worship is not a favor we do to God, nor an empty submission to His authority. Rather, God is due our thanksgiving and gratitude because He covered us, helped us, guarded

---

[125] In Psalm 136, David the prophet asks the people to give thanks (confess to the Lord). In this psalm, he lists the reasons of that thanksgiving, which are so many. For example, for He is good, who created, who made, who brought out the people...etc. He also composed whole psalms dedicated to giving thanks

us, accepted us to Himself, spared us, supported us, and has brought to this hour.

For He has covered us:

God knows very well what we have done, since nothing is hidden from Him. "Their ways are always in His sight; they are not hidden from His eyes" (Sirach 17:13). However, God cares about our image, so He reveals our virtues and hides our weaknesses. He puts a cover between the people and our sins and transgressions, so that others do not despise us. Being exposed to others might lead to despair; and despair might lead to more sin.

Nevertheless, we oftentimes abuse God's covering, mercy, kindness and defense, and fall into pride and haughtiness of heart. Not only that, but we start to judge others on their weaknesses, forgetting the plank in our own eyes and criticizing the speck in the eyes of others.

God may choose sometimes to expose rather than cover, only for the good of the person, when one remains on a destructive path and is in need of God's confrontation in order to be saved. Sometimes, we come around with subtle hints and God's kind covering, while other times, we continue in our way, which makes exposure suitable. This is why we must examine ourselves daily. It is the watchful person who says, "Though God did not confront me over my behavior today, and neither did anyone notice, I must not ignore the sin and drop my guard." The desert fathers say, "If we remember our sins, God forgets them, and if we forget them, God remembers them."

It is worthy of mentioning that oftentimes we complain when we are punished, or when we face any injustice or tribulation. We need to shift our mindset and remind ourselves that we got what we deserved justly, remembering the words of the thief on the cross, "And we indeed justly, for we receive the due reward of our deeds" (Luke 23:41). How many other times have we sinned in the past, yet neither God not others have convicted us?

God's covering can be resembled to a human eye; its beauty, color, and shape is admired by many, and through which the personality of man can be reveled. Examining the same eye closely, you will find a bluish ball filled with small veins, no beauty and no difference from all other eyes will be seen. God hides and covers what is not pleasant from within to show the beauty and the delight from without...now, what do you think about a beautiful eye that can't see? Or a body that looks healthy but suffers of tumors within?

Helped us and Supported us:

While sometimes a person just needs some help, other times, powerless, a person needs support, and requires God to carry the whole load; "Lord, I believe; help my unbelief!" (Mark 9:24).

God helps us when He adds more capabilities to ours, to assist, to reinforce, "He has helped His servant Israel, in remembrance of His mercy" (Luke 1:54). Other times, God supports and takes care of all; "the children have come to birth, but there is no strength to bring them forth" (2 Kings 19:3).

This reminds us of the beautiful story of "Footprints," where a person was walking in the desert and had asked God for help. Every few feet, he would look back and see four footprints, which reassured him that God is with him. After a while, the road became hard and he felt exhausted. When he looked back this time, he was surprised and saddened to see two footprints not four. At this moment, he complained and blamed God about how when he was able to walk, God was with him, but when he lost his energy, God left him. Instantly, he heard God's compassionate voice reassuring him that He did not abandon him, but the two footprints were God's not his. Initially, he just needed God's help and found it, but later, he needed someone to support him and lift him up entirely, and again, God did not hesitate.

God watches us as a compassionate father, and the moment we are in danger, he rushes to save us at the right time.

Guarded us:

We only know the hardships and the tribulations that we have been through, but we do not know that there were many more coming our way, but God has guarded us and dealt with these before they reached us; He sifted them! This applies to the tribulations from others as well as the wars of the devil, which God allows.

When the devil complained against Job, God allowed hardships to a certain extent. While the devil benefits from the concept of equality that God granted to all creatures, he still cannot do as he wills with whomever without control.

For instance, the air around us is loaded with microbes and viruses that can cause thousands of ordinary and dangerous diseases. Not catching them is not anyone's work, but it is the divine protection. Even those who get sick, they do in accordance with God's love and for their own good.

God draws a line and watches it, we can call it the danger line or the red line to disease, to sin, to harm...etc.

I remember a story about this young man who was driving his car through a busy street, filled with trees. While driving, one of those trees fell on the hood of his car. Although he was not hurt, he still murmured and complained questioning why this tree had to fall on his car and not someone else's. While everyone was overjoyed and thanked God that he is okay, he continued to complain about what happened to his car. He became preoccupied with evil thoughts rather than thoughts of gratitude towards God who guarded him.

Accepted us to Himself:

God accepted us as we are, with all the sin and defilement within us. He did not despise us, nor did He look at our impurities, just as the mother who bends down to pick up her crying child with raised expectant hands, and accepts him in her arms with unfathomable compassion, kissing him and consoling him, without paying any attention to any of his messiness. She loves him wholly, regardless of his state of appearance or cleanliness.

God himself uses the beautiful metaphor of a mother to describe His relationship with us. "As one whom his mother comforts, so I will comfort you" (Isaiah 66:13). "Can a woman forget her nursing child, and not have compassion on the son of her womb? Surely they may forget, yet I will not forget you" (Isaiah 49:15).

Motherhood is the highest of all instincts, truly miraculous. How much more would God be towards us? He is the One who instilled this compassion and love in all mothers. The devil knows this fact very well, but instills in us doubt towards God's love and compassion.

Our defilement and sin do not harm God, but it is us who get purified once we throw ourselves in His bosom. Does the sun get polluted if it shines upon a pile of garbage? Or does it purify it from bacteria? Likewise, if you get thoughts of having to repent first and get purified before entering the church, just think how would that happen away from church?! It is like a person goes in the sea to bathe; does the sea get polluted or does the person get cleansed?! Let us put God between us and our sins and defilements, and not let our sins separate us from Him.

Spared us:

God knows our nature, weakness, and lowliness, as He is the one who created us and formed us. When we sin, He defends us and finds excuses for us as we are targeted by the devil. He does not accept complaints against us, nor change His opinion of us, and would never withdraw from us.

God knows that we are weak and inclined to sin. "And the Lord said, 'My Spirit shall not strive with man forever, for he is indeed flesh'" (Genesis 6:3), This is not an exemption from responsibility, but rather out of His love, He spares us. Although Abraham, the father of nations, had lied to Pharaoh and the Egyptians, God did not abandon him, but rather defended him when he faced danger before Pharaoh (Genesis 12:11-20). This does not exempt us from responsibility, but God's discipline for us is between Him and us.

It is God's longsuffering and His sparing mercy that yielded thousands of saints. What if God had not spared Moses, the slave and murderer, Mary, the Egyptian harlot, and Saul the persecutor and Pharisee? We would have lost some of the most powerful examples of true repentance, holy purity and evangelical preaching in the history of our Church. Truly, God sees what will become of us, and not what we are now.

Brought us to this hour:

Perhaps the greatest gift God has given us is that we are still present until this moment. Some, whom we know, and others, whom we do not know, were among us last year, or just a few short months ago and now, they are not. Others were here even a few hours ago, but are not with us at this hour. As for us, He has brought us to this hour and has given us another chance to repent and return.

Oh how the dwellers of Hades hope for one of these days that we spend here! They marvel at how we waste years, months, and days from our lives just like that. The rich man, in the parable of Lazarus and the rich man, had realized this fact and even asked Abraham to do anything to save his family.

Just imagine if a chance were given to one of those in Hades to come back to life for a mere few days, what do you think they would do? Are not a few days enough to offer a pure repentance? This reminds me of a saintly monk, who, during his departure, while surrounded by the other monks, was found weeping. When they asked him about the reason for his weeping, he answered that he hopes that God may have patience and grant him more time. Astonished at his answer, for he was known for being a struggler and a saint, asked him how much time he desires to get before his departure. He answered, "I would like even one more day." They asked, "What would you do in that day?" He said, "If I'm not able to offer many things, it would be enough for me to spend the day weeping."

Likewise, it is possible for man to achieve a lot and be ahead of others in one hour, if he was active and fiery in his spirit. God grants each one twenty four hours as a daily allowance to invest and profit and make up for what is lost

Conclusion:

Thanksgiving in tribulation helps us overcome it. A life void of thanksgiving and submission leads to unbearable torment, while joy is the natural outcome of submission and thanksgiving.[126]

Thanksgiving is a sacrifice; "Whoever gives thanks, offers a gift of fine flour, and whoever acts with mercy, offers a sacrifice" (Sirach 35:4). The children of Israel used to continuously offer thanksgiving offerings as an expression of gratitude towards God (Leviticus 7:12 & Jeremiah 33:11).[127] "Let them sacrifice the sacrifices of thanksgiving, and declare His works with rejoicing" (Psalm 107:22).

"Continue earnestly in prayer, being vigilant in it with thanksgiving" (Colossians 4:2).

---

[126] See chapter "Life of Submission."

[127] The Eucharist is the sacrifice of thanksgiving, for the main prayer offered used to be called the thanksgiving prayer to God for creating the world with all that is in it.

www.ingramcontent.com/pod-product-compliance
Lightning Source LLC
LaVergne TN
LVHW011352080426
835511LV00005B/252